THE

HOLY SPIRIT

THE THIRD PERSON OF THE GODHEAD

Leonard MP Kayiwa

Unless otherwise indicated, all Scripture
quotations are taken from the
New King James version of the Bible,
and the old King James version

Formatted and typed by:
Pastor Gail B. Kayiwa, D.D. M.A. Urban Planning
and Policy Analysis, B.A Sociology and
Anthropology

Cover Design and Illustrations by:
Dr. Leonard Kayiwa
kayiwaministries@yahoo.com

The Holy Spirit; the Third Person of the Godhead
ISBN 978-0-9717609-4-3
Copyright ©2018 by Leonard MP Kayiwa

All rights reserved. Written permission must
Be secured from the publisher to use or
Reproduce any part of this book, except for
Brief quotations in critical reviews or
Articles. .
Printed in the United States of America

Leonard Kayiwa Ministries
P.O. Box 1898
Bolingbrook, Illinois 60440

Make Sure You Get to Know Who the Holy Spirit Is

THE
HOLY SPIRIT
LOVES
TO
GUIDE
YOU

Golden Rule No. 2

God

Will take you

As far

As

You are willing

To

Go

"if you are willing and obedient, you shall eat the good of the land; But if you refuse and rebel, you shall be devoured by the sword", For the mouth of the Lord has spoken."
Isaiah 1:19   nkjv Bible

Dedication

THIS BOOK IS DEDICATED
TO THE PEOPLE
IN
AFRICA, AMERICA
EUROPE, CHINA,
AUSTRALIA,
MIDDLE EAST, ETC.,
AND
TO ALL CHURCHES
AROUND THE WORLD
PLUS,
THOSE WHO HAVE WORKED
WITH ME
TO MAKE THE BOOK AVAILABLE
TO THE
NATIONS:
MY WIFE, DR. GAIL B. KAYIWA
AND MY CHILDREN
MOSES EMMANUEL KAYIWA
JOSHUA ISRAEL KAYIWA
ENOCH DEOGRACIOUS KAYIWA,
AND
MARY DEBORAH NAKAYIWA

ENDORSEMENTS

I WAS A MOSLEM BEFORE I MET BISHOP LEONARD KAYIWA IN 1994. HE WAS PREACHING A CRUSADE IN KAMWOKYA, UGANDA, AFRICA. THAT DAY I SAW MIRACLES AND WONDERS I HAD NEVER SEEN DURING MY ENTIRE LIFE. PEOPLE WERE HEALED OF DIABETES, AIDS, CANCER, BLOOD DISORDERS AND DEMONS LEFT PEOPLES' LIVES CRYING LOUDLY. AS A MOSLEM THEN, I WAS TAKEN BY SURPRISE, FOR THOSE KINDS OF THINGS WERE NOT HAPPENING IN OUR MOSQUES, BEING A STUDENT OF MEDICINE, AT MAKERERE UNIVERSITY THEN, I THOUGHT THAT WAS VERY UNUSUAL, SO I APPROACHED HIM AND ASKED HIM WHY ALL OF THESE MIRACLES COULD TAKE PLACE. THIS IS WHAT HE SAID TO ME, 'THE HOLY SPIRIT.' THAT DAY, I BECAME BORN AGAIN! THIS BOOK IN YOUR HAND IS A MIRACLE ITSELF,

ABRAHAM SSENYONEA, MD

We thank God for this book, everyone should read this book. This book should be on every table, every shelf, in every car, every plane and every church. God bless you.

BROTHER JOSEPH AUSTIN

DR. GAIL B. KAYIWA

I have watched very interesting things happen, when my husband, Bishop Leonard Kayiwa teaches about the Holy Spirit. It is as if the atmosphere changes to a tangible presence of God. In this book, God has given us, His children, help to get a better understanding of the Holy Spirit, and I assure you, the same anointing that shows up when he is preaching about the Third Person of the Godhead, is present on the pages of this book. I expect people to be filled with the Holy Spirit, with evidence of speaking in tongues, some will receive Jesus Christ as their Lord and Personal Savior, and many are going to be healed of various ailments, and the majority shall get their spiritual life enriched abundantly. Read it!

DR. GAIL B. KAYIWA, B.A., M.A., PROFESSIONAL GRANT WRITER   mrsrev3@gmail.com

What makes this book so unique is the level of the anointing that is experienced by all people, when Bishop Leonard Kayiwa is ministering. The anointing on his life and ministry literally breaks yolks and removes burdens. When I first met him, with his wife, in Dallas, Texas, while doing a crusade, I could sense something very powerful about him. He ministered the Word of God with boldness, love and compassion, and he was very Jesus centered. I saw miracles, wonders and signs that amazed me that day. I belonged to a certain religion, and there in, I never saw any such power present in our services, but that day, my life was changed and I chose Jesus as my Lord and Savior. This book lets you understand why that kind of power can manifest through a human being's life, I mean a person like you, and I want to let you know the force behind all of this is the Holy Spirit. After reading this book, my spiritual life has been so enriched and I have noticed supernatural things happening through me. Beloved, read this book prayerfully, it is a revelation given to us human beings through His servant, Leonard Kayiwa. You are going to move to another level in God. That is to another Glory, you are going to appreciate the Holy Spirit more.

Brother Gregory Anthony, PHD Mathematics

The subject of the Holy Spirit has been addressed with such accuracy which only an anointed vessel of God can do. Testimonies as well as scriptural quotations, make this book so relevant to all of us. God has sent us help. Let us receive it. This book clears confusion about the Third Person of the Godhead; the Holy Spirit. When you read it, you develop a desire to know the Spirit of God, as well as walk with Him in the journey of this life. The choice of words in this book is divinely. The author, Dr. Leonard Kayiwa, has literally taken us with him through an experience with the Holy Spirit, that brings you to one major conclusion: we all need the help of the Holy Spirit. This book lets you know that the Christian life is a gift of God, manifested in the lives of those who are ready to love Jesus Christ and the people of God. You will become a better soul winner, wiser in God, more compassionate, and full of hope, as a result of reading this book. God bless you.

P.S. Tell all of your friends and acquaintances to get a copy of this book, written by one of the most prolific writers of our time. A man of God born from Uganda, Africa Bishop Leonard Kayiwa.

Apostle Steven Bomgum

I wish I had come across a book like this in my early years of life. I belonged to a religion where they did not even know that the Holy Spirit exists, all they were talking about was a prophet. After some time, I met people who told me about Jesus Christ, and I became born again. All who knew me before wondered how I was able to leave that religion and become a born again Christian, even myself, I used to wonder. Well, I want to let you know; in this book you will find an answer to that: None other than 'the Holy Spirit!'

Dr. Mary Brown, Atomic Physics Scientist

THIS BOOK IS A MUST READ, I HAVE READ IT PRAYERFULLY AND THE ANOINTING OF GOD JUST CAME ALL OVER ME. THIS IS REAL! I WOULD LIKE TO TELL YOU MY BROTHER AND MY SISTER, THE BREATH OF GOD IS ON THIS BOOK, SOMEONE HAS TO GET BLESSED, IT IS FULL OF REVELATION KNOWLEDGE, SCRIPTURALLY SOUND AND VERY EASY TO UNDERSTAND. I HAVE OBTAINED COPIES FOR MANY OF MY FAMILY MEMBERS, AND I HAVE RECOMMENDED IT TO ALL OF MY FRIENDS. GOD HAS USED THE UNIQUENESS OF THIS MAN BORN IN THE NATION OF UGANDA, AFRICA, TO MAKE A POINT TO ALL OF US, THAT WE NEED TO KNOW THE HOLY SPIRIT. HIS EXPERIENCES WITH THE HOLY SPIRIT THAT HE HAS GENEROUSLY SHARED WITH US, MAKES THIS WORK SO PRECIOUS AND HELPFUL TO ANY READER. IT IS FULL OF TESTIMONIES AND REAL LIFE EVENTS, THAT ARE DRAWN FROM SITUATIONS AS, THE BISHOP MINISTERS IN DIFFERENT COUNTRIES AND CONTINENTS. WHEN YOU READ THE BOOK, YOU JUST FEEL THAT YOU ARE PART OF THE SERVICES. THIS IS EXACTLY THE KIND OF EXPERIENCE YOU WILL HAVE WHILE READING THIS BOOK. IT IS AS IF YOU ARE IN A LIVE SERVICE, FULL OF THE POWER OF GOD, AND THE WORD BEING TAUGHT UNDER REVELATION KNOWLEDGE.

Brother/Professor Charles, PhD ORAL ROBERTS UNIVERSITY, HARVARD UNIVERSITY, PRINCETON UNIVERSITY

FORWARD

IT IS GOD'S WILL FOR YOU TO BE EQUIPPED

The Bible says in the Book of Amos, Chapter Three, Verse Three, "Can two walk together, unless they are agreed?" Amos 3:3 Beloved, I believe this is one of the most eye opening scriptures in regard to your walk with God, you will ever find in the Bible.

We all need the miracles of God, we want to experience His power, we desire to see people healed, delivered and blessed, especially many of us who are soul winners. We don't want to lay hands on the sick and nothing happens, nor do we want to tell the devils to leave, and they just sit as well as stand there laughing at us. We want to do better than that, just talking with no power involved.

In my experience operating in the miraculous with God's power present to levels that even cause me to tremble, I mean when the presence of God is so strong that everyone in the service is vibrating under the anointing, and the people are being tremendously blessed, I have come to conclude that the only answer to that is the way we treat the Holy Spirit.

We have to refrain from anything that would grieve the Spirit of God, we have to abandon talks and behaviors that are not in line with the Word of God. We have to be Jesus centered. People whose desire is to glorify the Lord Jesus Christ, in our entire lifestyle.

Things don't just happen. A human being can't force God to do anything for him, the only way to come into God's presence, is His way. We need a guide, we need a helper, we need one, who is called "Himself" to help us know the things of God. One, who is one with God; and that one is The Third Person of the Godhead; The Holy Spirit.

God commanded me to write this book and He said, it will to go to all people and those who will be willing to know more about the Holy Spirit will experience divine change in their lives and carry out great exploits.

Your Brother in Christ,
Bishop Leonard Kayiwa, D.D.

DR. BISHOP LEONARD MP KAYIWA

ABOUT THE AUTHOR

Dr. Leonard Kayiwa is a highly anointed servant of God, he started ministering before the Lord, early in life. An altar boy at nine years old, he served at St. Peter's Cathedral at Nsambya, Kampala, Uganda, Africa. He would serve in every mass, almost every day.

His love for God began early. After finishing primary school at St. Peter's Primary, he joined St. Henry's College Kitovu, Masaka, Uganda, where God blessed him with very high marks in school, whereby he could devote a lot of his time helping his fellow students in whatever subject they needed help in. God gifted him, especially in mathematics, physics, chemistry, history, technical drawing and Biblical studies.

He joined Makerere University in Kampala, Uganda where "he got born again", which resulted in a drastic change in his life. He did Irrigation and Water Conservation Engineering at Hahai University in Nanjing, China and received the Baptism of the Holy Spirit with evidence of speaking in tongues in Hong Kong, at the new Covenant Church. God does unusual miracles through his life and many have become "born again" through his ministry.

TABLE OF CONTENTS

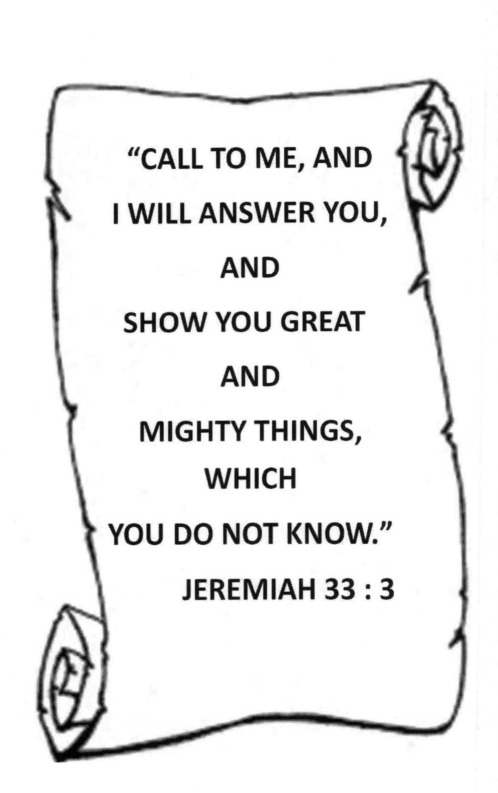

"CALL TO ME, AND

I WILL ANSWER YOU,

AND

SHOW YOU GREAT

AND

MIGHTY THINGS,

WHICH

YOU DO NOT KNOW."

JEREMIAH 33 : 3

"BUT THE HELPER

THE

HOLY SPIRIT

WHOM

THE FATHER WILL SEND

IN MY NAME

HE

WILL TEACH YOU

ALL

THINGS

AND BRING

TO

YOUR REMEMBRANCE

ALL

THINGS

THAT I SAID TO YOU"

JOHN 14:26

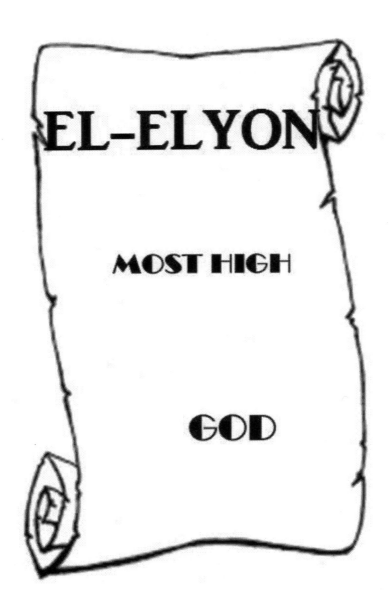

EL-ELYON

MOST HIGH

GOD

1

KNOWING
THE HOLY SPIRIT
The Pathway to God's Power

"But you shall receive power, when the Holy Spirit has come upon you; and you shall be witnesses to Me; in Jerusalem and in all Judea and Samaria, and to the end of the earth." Acts 1:8

We are living in perilous times, amidst us are weapons of mass destruction. High caliber guns are in the hands of so many people. Extremism ideologies are easily communicated through very many channels on the social media. Our children are under intense pressure; for so much is thrown at them, in the disguise of knowledge. Shooters have found their way to schools, and have inflicted pain and death on our children.

These days, when you see someone with a gun, you naturally have to be on high alert, for we have been told

The Holy Spirit; the Third Person of the Godhead

that some of the gun holders might be having mental problems, whereby they can go off and start shooting at anything moving. With all of that happening, one wonders who to turn to for help. So many solutions have been offered to us by various sources, but they don't seem to work satisfactorily. It seems that the problem is deeper than what has been diagnosed. Some times what is referred to as love, is not at all in that vicinity; it is altogether lust! Even, food has been so compromised that one spends their hard earned money on some fast food that lacks the nutrients to sustain their bodies, which makes them vulnerable to all kinds of malfunction, as well as depressions and illnesses.

All of these challenges are having a lot of toll on human beings, the result is anger, bitterness; "Now the works of the flesh are evident, which are adultery, fornication, uncleanness, lewdness, idolatry, sorcery, hatred, contentious, jealousies, outbursts of wrath, selfish ambitions, dissensions, heresies, envy, murders, drunkenness, revelries, and the like of which I tell you beforehand, Just as I also told you in times past, that those who practice such things will not inherit the Kingdom of God." Gal 5:19-21

In this book, God has sent me to talk to you about the Holy Spirit; the third person of the God Head. You and I are taking this flight together, we are going to take off like an eagle and we will soar and fly very high. "Have you not known? Have you not heard? The everlasting God, the LORD. The Creator of the ends of the earth. Neither faints nor is weary. His understanding is unsearchable. He gives power to the weak, And to those who have no might He increases strength. Even the youth shall faint and be weary, And the young men shall utterly fail, But those who wait on the LORD shall renew their strength; they shall mount up with wings like eagles; They shall run and not be weary. They shall walk and not faint." Is 40:28-31

I am writing this book under a very strong anointing, the Holy Spirit, Himself is helping us; me and you, as the Lord God unveils revelation knowledge about this very important subject. You could be experiencing a Holy presence right now as you are reading; it is God's presence. Your life is changing drastically for the better at this moment, for the entrance of His word brings light, "The entrance of your word gives light; it gives understanding to the simple." Ps 119:130 God is touching you, He is moving you from glory to glory, for it is time for great exploits; God wants to reveal Himself

The Holy Spirit; the Third Person of the Godhead

Strong through your life. Your quest to know more about the Holy Spirit is being rewarded right now. The power of God is upon you for miracles, wonders and signs, and the eyes of God almighty are on you right now. "For the eyes of the LORD run to and fro throughout the whole earth, to show Himself strong on behalf of those whose heart is loyal to Him." 2 Chr 16:9 Your heart is loyal to the Lord God Almighty, that is why you have this book in your possession. Please read it prayerfully, for when you are blessed we all benefit from that blessing.

Unusual Manifestation of God's Presence Takes Place as I Teach about the Holy Spirit, in the City of St. Louis, Missouri, USA

I was invited to preach in an indoor crusade in the City of St. Louis, Missouri, U.S.A. The event was very well promoted on radio, in church bulletins, and on T.V. stations. Very nice flyers had been printed inviting people to the services. This took place around 2004. I had never been in that city before. The organizers made sure all people are invited, irrespective of their religious affiliations. We had this crusade in a very nice building, it was a former Catholic Church Cathedral, that had been bought by an evangelical church. There was ample parking for everyone.

The people were told that a Bishop from Uganda, East Africa, would be ministering, and that he has a proven ministry of miracles, signs and wonders following as he preaches the Gospel of our Lord Jesus Christ. They were also introduced to one of the books that I wrote, 'Ministering to God, Key to a Prosperous Life, Church filled with God's Power, Miracles, Wonders and Signs.' These people were ready for the move of God. A large number of pastors decided to come; some from different states. We flew into St. Louis and we were met at the airport by very expectant hosts, they were expecting miracles, wonders, and signs: they were in a prayerful mode, we all prayed in the Holy Spirit, all the way to the place of our abode. The presence of the Lord God Almighty was all over us.

The Lord Instructs me to Minister about the Holy Spirit

I was in my room praying for the service that day, when suddenly, through inner witness, the Lord God let

The Holy Spirit; the Third Person of the Godhead

me know that He wanted the message to be about the Holy Spirit. "Who is the Holy Spirit?" As usual, I was prepared to say what He wanted me to speak, as well as teach, what He gives me to teach, for that is; what is the reason for the manifestation of God's glory in tangible form in our worship services throughout the world. This is affirmative to the words of God to Prophet Jeremiah in the Holy Bible. "Then said I: 'Ah, Lord' God! Behold I cannot speak, for I am a youth." But the LORD said to me: "Do not say; 'I am a youth.' For you shall go to all to whom I send you, And whatever I command you, you shall speak, Do not be afraid of their faces, for I am with you to deliver you." Says the Lord." Jer 1:6-8

When you preach what the Lord gives you to share with His people, the Glory of God is revealed in various forms; revelation knowledge, miracles, wonders and signs. Here I am talking about the Rhema Word: That Is, a word for the season, something God wants to be delivered to those particular people at that particular time. Well, it is always better to obey the Lord. Always remember that, obedience is greater than sacrifice, and if we are to experience the supernatural, we have to be

Knowing the Holy Spirit: The Pathway to God's Power

willing to be led by the Spirit of God, "For as many as are led by the Spirit of God, these are sons of God." Rom 8:14

The Glory of the Lord Revealed as the Word Goes Forth.

The crusade location was packed to capacity. A good number of ministers had already taken their places on the podium. These pastors, evangelists, teachers, prophets, and apostles, had come from different denominations: Baptist, Church of God in Christ Episcopal Churches, Methodist Churches, Catholic Churches, Church of Christ, Pentecostals…etc. These ministers were hungry for God's word. I could sense it. "Blessed are those who hunger and thirst for righteousness, For they shall be filled." Matt 5:6 Those words are from our Lord Jesus Christ, to everyone who hungers for righteousness. No wonder God moved me by His Spirit to teach on the subject of the Holy Spirit for He wanted to bless His people.

The worship was amazing! I had asked the host pastor to get me a team of very anointed worshippers. People who could pay as well as sing songs that bless

The Holy Spirit; the Third Person of the Godhead

The Lord God, songs like: Alleluia, Alleluia.....; Oh Lord My God when I in awesome wonder..........How Great Thou Art...; Glory, Glory, Glory to the Lamb...; Holy Spirit Thou Art Welcome in this Place, Omnipotent Father, of mercy and grace......; He Touched Me......,etc. were presented to the congregation. The people of God were in total agreement at worshipping and praising God along with the choir. I was standing about two meters away from the pulpit, when I felt the presence of God all over me. It was electrical-like; it was a very beautiful Holy Presence. I knew in my heart it was time to deliver the message of God.

In the Book of First Chronicles, Chapter Fourteen, from verse thirteen to verse sixteen, God gives David and the whole army of Israel, marching orders, that would lead to the defeat of the invading armies – the Philistines. "Then the Philistines once again made a raid on the Valley. Therefore, David inquired again of God, and God said to him, "You shall not go up after them; circle around them, and come upon them in front of the mulberry trees. "And it shall be, when you hear a sound of marching in the tops of the mulberry trees, then you shall go out to battle, for God has gone out before you to strike the camp of the Philistines." So David did as God commanded him, and they drove back the armies of the Philistines from Gibeon as far as Gezer." 1 Chr 14:13-16

Action following the presence of God's power

People had come from everywhere, to hear the Word of God preached. Some needed urgent healings; their lives needed to be free from diseases and demonic torments. Others were dealing with the challenge of debts; they wanted a miracle of debt cancellation or supernatural wisdom to obtain finances to pay off debt. Others needed to become "Born Again." Some were seeking God for the Baptism of the Holy Spirit with evidence of speaking in tongues; many wanted the joy of the Lord back in their lives; and restoration of peace in their relationships.

Pastors wanted power back in their church services, this was a crusade, we were to force the enemy to give up what it had stolen, as well as going at anything that

The Holy Spirit; the Third Person of the Godhead

Was against God's people. We had to defeat the thief "The thief does not come except to steal and to kill and to destroy; I have come that they may have life and that they may have it more abundantly." John 10:10 When I arrived in St. Louis Missouri, before the crusade began, they interviewed me on a live radio program about miracles, wonders and signs that I have seen God perform in the course of my ministry around the world. Many people called in with very interesting questions; some even wondered whether the miracles of our Lord Jesus Christ are for the church today. Well, I encouraged them to attend the crusade and experience, as well as partake of those miraculous divine interventions by God Almighty.

Beloved, even right now God Almighty is touching you. His power is present to bring a fundamental change in your circumstances; receive your miracle now in the Name of Jesus Christ of Nazareth. God is doing something for you, which is only possible through the mighty deliverance arm of His. It is happening right now! This power is yoke breaking, burden removing, and does slay demons!

Knowing the Holy Spirit: The Pathway to God's Power

The Lord is telling me that some of you reading this book, have never had a tangible encounter with the power of God, well these writings carry an anointing from the Lord God Almighty to cause you to move from Glory to Glory. The presence of God, by the Spirit of God, is operational, right now in your life. Anything which has been trying to hold you back from knowing the person of the Holy Spirit, is being taken out of your way now, in the Name of Jesus Christ. God is not the author of confusion. Any confusion that would have been cast upon you through erroneous teaching in regard to the Holy Spirit, I destroy it right now, with the fire of God. I decree and declare that you will live to your destiny in the Lord God Almighty, and that exploits shall be done through your life, and many people will be helped through your obedience to the Word of God.

I Step to the Pulpit Amidst the Power of God

When I felt that glorious presence of God on me, and all around the sanctuary, I knew that it was time to flow with the Holy Spirit. As you are aware, at the beginning of this chapter, the scripture quotation is,

The Holy Spirt; the Third Person of the Godhead

"But you shall receive power when the Holy Spirit has come upon you; and you shall be witnesses......." Acts 1:8. I opened the Bible and began teaching about the Holy Spirit. I went precept upon precept, line upon line, a little here and a little there, comparing spiritual thins with spiritual things, "These things we also speak not in words which man's wisdom teaches, but which the Holy Spirit teaches, comparing spiritual things with spiritual." I Cor 2:13. I went on for half an hour, suddenly the Lord God started giving me words of knowledge for people's healings in the audience.

I called out ten persons through Word of Knowledge: this is one of the gifts of the Holy Spirit, whereby some information is revealed to a child of God divinely by God Almighty concerning the present situation or pointing to a place or something presently happening in somebody's life. This kind of grace evokes faith in a person, they tend to realize that God knows everything about them and does care.

They came to the altar. What amazed everyone, is this; when I pointed my finger at them and said, "the

Knowing the Holy Spirit: The Pathway to God's Power

Holy Spirit is upon you, in the Name of Jesus Christ and the Power of God is descending upon you to remove those sicknesses, diseases and infirmities." Those ten people were swept off their feet by that visibly on them Power: The Power of God was going through them like a live electrical current, without me touching them at all. These people were healed instantly, the pain left them. They checked themselves and the pain had gone. Some who had tumors, they disappeared; back pain gone; tumors in the stomach gone, migraine headaches gone, chest pain gone. This was a very crucial eye opening moment for all the ministers in attendance, for I was teaching about the Holy Spirit when this amazing power came into manifestation.

The power of God was beautifully present, that when I asked the people to lift their hands, to receive a touch from the Lord God Almighty, people could not wait, their hands were already up expecting a touch from God, the power of God surged through the entire congregation. The people of God became blessed bountifully, many received Jesus Christ as their personal Savior on that day for the first time. It was like

The Holy Spirit; the Third Person of the Godhead

what happened in the Book of Acts, Chapter Sixteen, when God manifested His power in the jail cells of Philippi that led the jailer to ask what he needed to do to be saved. "But at midnight Paul and Silas were praying and singing hymns to God, and the prisoners were listening to them. Suddenly, there was a great earthquake, so that the foundations of the prison were shaken; and immediately all the doors were opened and everyone's chains were loosed. And the keeper of the prison, awaking from sleep and seeing the prison doors open, supposing the prisoners had fled, drew his sword and was about to kill himself. But Paul called with a loud voice saying, "Do yourself no harm for we are all here." Then he called for a light, ran in, and fell down trembling before Paul and Silas. And he brought them out and said, 'Sirs, what must I do to be saved?' So they said, "Believe on the Lord Jesus Christ, and you will be saved, you and your household." Acts 16:25-30

People Respond to Salvation

People who had come accompanying those who were born again but they were yet to receive Jesus Christ as their personal Savior; that day on seeing what had happened, gladly came on the front to become 'Born Again.' Many lined up to receive the Baptism of the Holy Spirit with evidence of speaking in tongues, others the Holy Spirit came upon them right where they were seated in the pews and started speaking in the heavenly language – tongues. The preachers at the podium were so blessed by God's presence; the power of God was all over them. It was glorious! It was as if God was telling all of us that I want you to know who the Holy Spirit is: there was joy amidst the people of God that day.

A Man Testifies That Something That was Seated on Him on the Left Shoulder, with its invisible hand wrapped around his neck, causing unbearable pain: That, that day, its grip on him was broken and its presence was no more on him

There was a man who came in the crusade on the invitation of his friend, this man was around 65 years of age. He said that it seems something would be seated on his left shoulder, and it was as if it had a hand around

The Holy Spirit; the Third Person of the Godhead

his neck. He continued to explain that this started two years ago, he went to his doctor and they examined him, but they could not find what was causing that discomfort on his shoulders and neck. They did all X-rays, but they were not able to see anything irregular, so they resorted to putting him on pain medication, as well as sending him to therapy.

This man was also given an electrical device to help with massaging his neck. He went to his pastor and told him that he knows something invisible is tormenting him. It is like an invisible monkey seated on his shoulders with a hand around his neck. Well, they prayed for him, but nothing happened. This attack of this invisible thing, was about to drive him crazy. He told us that in his church, they don't flow in the power of God like what he saw that day. He testified further that during the worship and praise at the beginning of the service, he started feeling like fire was coming on him, something he had never felt before, during his entire life. He knew that something good was happening to him.

Suddenly, the power of God hit him, like a bolt of

Knowing the Holy Spirit: The Pathway to God's Power

Lightening, and he felt a snap around his neck, it was like something was supernaturally removed off his left shoulder, the weight of that invisible thing was gone and he became free after two years of torment. This man was full of joy, praising the Lord God Almighty. Thanking Jesus for his deliverance. He asked me, if I would pray for him, to receive the Baptism of the Holy Spirit with evidence of speaking in tongues. I could see that his faith was already high, and he was ready for a change. The moment I said to him, receive the Baptism of the Holy Spirit, the Lord Jesus Christ filled him with the Holy Spirit, with evidence of speaking in tongues. This man spoke in tongues for nearly ten minutes nonstop. Everybody in the congregation was blessed at the manifestation of that man's miracle.

Beloved, this joy is available to you right now. I speak to anything that has been limiting your understanding of the Holy Spirt of God; to get out of your way, now; may your knowledge of the Holy Spirit of God increase as you continue with me on this journey in this book, about, "The Holy Spirit." I am being blessed, along with you right now! Be blessed right now

The Holy Spirit; the Third Person of the Godhead

The Holy Spirit is present with you right now and as it happened to Paul and Silas at the Philippi Jail, God is swinging doors open for you to enlarge your fellowship with the Holy Spirit and to bring you in the place of being an effective witness of the death and resurrection of our Lord Jesus Christ.

We need the Holy Spirit's help, we need to know what He likes so that we flow in His power, "And do not grieve the Holy Spirit of God by whom you were sealed for the day of redemption." Eph 4:30

The Holy Spirit Saves Samson from being Eaten by a Lion

In the book of Judges, we have a very interesting story of a man called Samson. He happened to be one of the Judges of Israel, he is one of the persons in the Old Testament who was sealed with the Holy Spirit, like us in the New Testament. Samson was called by God to bring the children of Israel out of the oppression of the Philistines; like you and me, God has commissioned us to preach the Gospel-His good news, to all people, to the ends of the earth; that is everywhere.

Knowing the Holy Spirit: The Pathway to God's Power

"And Jesus came and spoke to them saying, "All authority has been given to Me in heaven and on earth. "Go therefore and make disciples of all the nations, baptizing them in the Name of the Father and of the Son and of the Holy Spirit. "teaching them to observe all things that I have commanded you; and lo, I am with you always, even to the end of the age." Amen" Matt 28:18-20

Like Samson, we are not operating in a very friendly environment. Samson on his way to Timnah met an unexpected enemy. "So Samson went down to Timnah with his father and mother and came to the vineyard of Timnah. Now to his surprise, a young lion came roaring against him." Jud 14:5. This lion did not care whether Samson was a servant of God, and that it was of the Lord for Samson to go down to Timnah. "But his father and mother did not know that it was of the LORD – that He was seeking an occasion to move against the Philistines. For at that time the Philistines had dominion over Israel." Jud 14:4 This young lion desired to eat Samson; it did not know the extent of divine help he had through the Holy Spirit. Possibly it had attacked

The Holy Spirit; the Third Person of the Godhead

Other human beings before and prevailed over them. The following verse is very revealing about why we need to know the Holy Spirit by whom we were sealed for the day of redemption; that day when you need to be debt free, healed, delivered from demonic oppression, saved from accidents, pulled out of the fowler's snare, shielded from sorcery and witchcraft, as well as some evil persons. The Bible says; in that bad situation of Samson, that someone helped him, "And the Spirit of the LORD came mightily upon him, and he tore the lion apart as one would have torn apart a young goat, though he had nothing in his hand. But he did not tell his father or his mother what he had done." Jud 14:6

Precious one; The Holy Spirit. We need to know this third person of the God Head. It is He, who manifested those healings in the crusade I conducted in the Name of Jesus Christ, in St. Louis, Missouri, U.S.A. and many gave their lives to Jesus Christ. It is the Holy Spirit that saved Samson from the paw of a hungry, angry lion. Whatever demons were stirring up that creature, to rage at a man on a divine mission from God, they were rendered powerless. This kind of operation

The Holy Spirit: The Pathway to God's Power

is taking place for you now; you are being energized supernaturally to know more and receive more from the Lord. The presence of God is all around you. God is leading you to go further in the knowledge of Him, for He is doing you good right now.

Paul and Barnabas Prevails Over the Sorcerer due to the Help of the Holy Spirit

In the book of Acts Chapter Thirteen, we run into a very tricky situation. Paul and Barnabas had been commissioned by the Holy Spirit to go and preach the Gospel to the perishing world; this took place as the people in the church were fasting and praying. "As they ministered to the Lord and fasted, the Holy Spirit said, "Now separate to Me Barnabas and Saul for the work to which I have called them." Then having fasted and prayed, and laid hands on them, they sent them away. So being sent out by the Holy Spirit, they went down to Seleucia and from there they sailed to Cyprus." Acts 13:2-4

Here you notice that the Holy Spirit has a direct role in the carrying out of the Great Commission that was

The Holy Spirit; the Third Person of the Godhead

given to the Believers by the second person of the Godhead, Jesus Christ. Further, what makes it very important for us to know Him, is the fact that in the course of carrying out the call they were assigned to; the Holy Spirit stayed with them throughout all the challenges they faced. One of them was sorcerer, a false prophet, a Jew whose name was Bar-Jesus. This man operated and functioned in witchcraft and spells. He was in the way of their efforts to win souls, this man resisted them seeking to turn the proconsul they were ministering to away from the faith-But the Holy Spirit! "Then Saul, who also is called Paul, filled with the Holy Spirit, looked intently at him and said, "O full of all deceit and all fraud, you son of the devil, you enemy of all righteousness, will you not cease perverting the straight ways of the Lord? "And now, indeed the hand of the Lord is upon you, and you shall be blind, not seeing the sun for a time." And immediately a dark mist fell on him, and he went around seeking someone to lead him by the hand." Acts 13:9-11

There is no way these precious Apostles would have prevailed over this witch; this one was a psychic, a palm reader, evil possessed, a sorcerer, if it wasn't the divine intervention of the Holy Spirit. No wonder we need to know who He is. Demons are there; sorcerers are out there very busy casting spells on people and their belongings, as well as their finances. We need the power of the Holy Spirit to stop them from hindering our progress as well as destroying the lives of God's people. That is why God Almighty led me to write this book.

We just cannot risk being powerless, when we are faced by this kind of wicked disasters. We need to be filled with the Holy Spirit. The church in the book of Acts functioned in the Holy Spirit, it was a church of miracles, wonders and signs. Works of the devil were being destroyed, healings occurred everywhere, brotherly love was on the increase; the believers strived to be on one accord in Jesus Christ. These people knew the Holy Spirit, and they endeavored to follow His leading. "For as many as are led by the Spirit of God, these are the Sons of God. For you did not receive the spirit of bondage again to fear, but you received the Spirit of adoption by whom we cry out "Abba, Father." The Spirit Himself bears witness with our spirit that we are children of God." Romans 8:14-16

The Holy Spirit; the Third Person of the Godhead

Every reasonable person would want to know the will of God for their lives, we really desire to follow a holy, God laid out path. For in all of us, God put a witness that there is something better and worth aspiring to, for we were made in the image of God. At this juncture, let us examine this supernatural leading in the context of bearing witness.

The Holy Spirit Bears Witness with our Spirits that we are Sons of God

I have been in ministry for a long time. God has had me start churches with one person to begin with. These churches eventually grew up and many ended up converted to Christianity; they became, 'Born Again Believers'. I have counselled as well as prayed with a lot of people, concerning various issues. Some of the challenges they were up against, were very tough, only God could resolve them. Some would be marital issues, financial concerns, legal matters, others were sicknesses like: cancer, diabetes, pneumonia, Aids, etc. God has enabled me to cast out many evil spirits that had intruded in people's lives; I have witnessed amazing healings and deliverances, through the power of the Holy Spirit, in the Name of our Lord, Jesus Christ. One amazing thing that has stood out clearly is the fact that, those persons, even though they could be up against insurmountable situations; they still strongly confessed that they are God's children. They tend to have that witness in them of who they are, a proof that there is a supernatural impartation within their hearts regarding their identity, from God Himself.

A Woman Maintains her Testimony by the Help of the Holy Spirit, that she is a Child of God and Gets her Store Back

I knew this lady early in the beginning of my call to ministry, she happened to be a believer. Her husband had passed away, so she had to take care of four children. She and her husband had run a store front business in the City of Kampala, Uganda, in East Africa. It was the kind of a shop where various items were sold. This lady had great faith. She had received Jesus Christ as her personal Savior and

The Holy Spirit; the Third Person of the Godhead

openly talked about Christ, but it happened that some people wanted to take away her livelihood. The objective of those people was to take away the building at which her store and apartment were located. This kind of buildings were allocated to certain persons by The Uganda Custodial Board, that managed the disposal of those properties to people whom they deemed would run businesses in them so that they don't become depleted, and that some revenue be obtained for the city.

The people who were corruptly maneuvering to take away the property of that widow, a Believer; they had an upper hand in the entire matter, looking at it from the natural. They used threats, as well as intimidation, expecting her to pack up and leave. They also knew some people on the Custodian Board, and were corruptly telling them that this woman was a widow and had no business owning the apartment and the store front. Somebody tried to start a fire at that property, which the lady and the people around her, helped to put out. It was like an electrical short circuit with no proper explanation how those wires came apart. In the process of putting the fire out, this precious widow woman suffered burns on both of her hands.

The Widow Woman Prevails Against her Foes through the Testimony of the Holy Spirit

What was extraordinary about this situation, was the testimony of this lady; this lady's argument to the board of directors of the custodian board was, 'I am a child of God, and God Almighty will help me keep my shop and apartment, even though my husband is deceased.' Well, they informed her that, 'You do not have enough money to maintain that property, nor enough items to keep the business going; there is someone else who wants to take over that property and have a lot of money.' This woman answered back and said, "I am a child of God and a widow, I have four children for whom I am paying school fees to stay in school. God is not going to allow you to take our livelihood away from us." And she would quote to them Psalms Sixty-Eight, verse five. "A father of the fatherless, a defender of widows, Is God in His holy habitation." Ps. 68:5 This lady was a warrior in Christ, and an intercessor.

The Holy Spirit; the Third Person of the Godhead

When this dear woman argued her case, it sounded crazy to them. Her assailants tried their best to undermine her credibility, portraying her as a crazy person. Letters to evict her were sent to her business location. These people tried many tricks to run her off of the property. I would pass by to find out what she was going to do, but she maintained her testimony, even with tears streaming down her face; that no one was going to remove her from that property, for she is a child of God.

This lady, in her sixties had unmovable witness by the Holy Spirit, that she was a child of God and a joint heir with Christ Jesus. "and if children, heirs- then heirs of God and joint heirs with Christ, if indeed we suffer with Him that we may also be glorified together." Rom 8:17

These were my early days in ministry, it was around 1992, my faith in God was increasing; just hearing what this precious Saint was confessing. The Name of Jesus Christ was strong on her lips. She could pray loudly at her shop, in the Name of Jesus Christ, and interestingly enough, she had the faith to receive her miracle. This precious widow was very confident in God. She told everyone around her, even her foes; that they won't be able to drive her and her children out of their store and apartment. Precious reader of this book: The Holy Spirit, we need to know Him. Her confidence was divine, she had a supernaturally imparted witness about who she was, and whose she is. "Now this is the confidence that we have in Him, that if we ask anything according to His will, He hears us. And if we know that He hears us, whatever we ask, we know that we have the petitions that we have asked of Him." I John 5:14-15

I have a word for you.

You have a confidence, a witness in your heart concerning something you talked to God about in the Name of Jesus Christ; you know deep in you that you are a child of God: you have a peace that surpasses understanding regardless of the contrary circumstances around you. The Lord God is telling me to tell you right now, that this persuasion is from Him, for it is the Holy Spirit bearing witness with your spirit that you are a recipient of that miracle from God. So, please do not

The Holy Spirit; the Third Person of the Godhead

cast away your confidence, "Therefore do not cast away your confidence, which has great reward. For you have need of endurance, so that after you have done the will of God, you may receive the promise." Heb 10:35-36

As I am writing this book, the Third Person of the Godhead; The Holy Spirit, is showing me that, a number of you are receiving a desire to know more of Him. You love Jesus Christ, you appreciate the fact that He died for you on the rugged cross at Calvary, and you want to do anything He asks of you. You want to be a witness of His death and resurrection to a dying world, you desire to lay hands on the sick, and they be healed. You have the compassion of God in your heart for those who are being tormented as well as under the influence demonic spirits; you want an effective prayer life, whereby you pray according to the will of God.

You are tired of being tired, and fed up of being fed up. You no longer want powerless religions. You are no longer interested in rituals and religious routines; you want the real deal, well you are on the right path; the path to the power of God through knowing the Holy Spirit. God has you and I for miracles, wonders and signs. "Here am I and the children whom the LORD has given me! We are for signs and wonders in Israel from the LORD of hosts, who dwells in Mount Zion." Is 8:18

let Us Continue on the Widow's Victory

Now, as the scuffle continued between those who were scheming to take away the property from this woman of faith, and her precious children, God suddenly gave a word to this lady. A word was dropped in her Spirit by the Holy Spirit of God, to write a letter to the minister in charge of all those departments that she was having trouble with. In America, that minister would be referred to as Secretary of commerce. They are appointed by presidents the nations. They do have executive powers.

Amazingly enough, the minister received the letter and moved very fast, he contacted the custodian board in regard to this 'Born Again', confessing to be child of God, believer, and asked for a review of the decision they had taken.

A miracle in making

Beloved, a review was made and a decision was reach-

The Holy Spirit; the Third Person of the Godhead

ed to let the lady keep the building; the jokers fled, and an order was entered restraining them from bothering this precious widow and to stay away from her premise. This lady was known as a Jesus person. She could praise the Lord Jesus Christ and testify of what the Lord God had done for he publicly. She often said that with God all things are possible. "For with God nothing will be impossible." Luke 1:37

Beloved of God, the Holy Spirit empowered, this seemingly powerless woman, compared to her foes, with divine God ideas and wisdom; it was like the situation of Mary when she was to bring forth a savior. Mary had no husband, she knew no man carnally, one would wonder how she would conceive; well, the answer was with the Holy Spirit. "…The Holy Spirit will come upon you, and the power of the Highest will overshadow you; therefore, also, that Holy one who is born will be called the Son of God." Luke 1:35

The testimony of that lady, a widow, and a mother of four children, whose husband had passed away, was part of the platform that launched me into a ministry of faith with miracles, wonders and signs following. There is no way that she would prevail over her assailants, who seemed to have no regard for God, without the help of the third person of the Godhead – the Holy Spirit. I am going to get into deep teaching with you about the Holy Spirit, just make sure you don't fall off the train. This journey is very interesting; so much is unfolding right now, following God's leading in the writings of this book. This book will find its way to millions of people all over the world, and lives will be changed tremendously for better, and great victories shall be attained for the Kingdom of God. The Lord God Almighty commanded me to write this script; this magnificent work for you and many others.

The relevance of the scriptures then and now, in regard to the present challenges

God has enabled me to council a lot of people, there are times when I used to pray for and pray with almost thirty different people every day. The anointing of God would be present strong, and healing power of God flowing, due to that, people through the word of mouth would invite others to come for prayer at our church. There were about twenty ushers and ministers working

The Holy Spirit; the Third Person of the Godhead

with me. These men and women who are today pastors, prophets, evangelists, apostles, teachers and intercessor were no strangers to the power of God. During the counselling sessions, God Almighty would show me scriptures in the Bible to give to His people. You might argue and say that these scriptures, especially in the Old Testament, and epistles were for those people at that time, which is true, though there is more to it in regard to the operation of the Holy Spirit.

The Holy Bible was written under the inspiration of the Holy Spirit. It is infallible with God's breath on it. The same Holy Spirit who caused the Word to come to those people of that time, still sometimes takes the same word and cause it to become alive for our benefit today. It is like you taking your name and replacing it with someone else's name, causing that word to become personal to you. No wonder there is no other book in the world like the Holy Bible. The scriptures come alive in regard to our circumstances, due to the witness of the Holy Spirit. I have seen God using simple phrases from the Bible and change lives. Make sure you take time to read as well as meditate on scriptures, for the entrance of His words brings light. "The entrance of Your words gives light; it gives .....' Ps 119:130

Knowing the Holy Spirit: The Pathway to God's Power

You are going to come across a number of scriptures quoted in this book in regard to this very, very relevant subject: The Holy Spirit, the Third Person of the Godhead. These scriptures are applicable in our lives now and they should be handled with all due diligence.

Jesus Commands them not to depart from Jerusalem, but to wait for the promise of the Father

In the Book of Acts, Chapter One, Verse Four, the disciples were assembled together, and our resurrected Savior appeared to them, and gave then a divine command, "And being assembled together with them. He commanded them not to depart from Jerusalem, but to wait for the promise of the Father. "Which," He said, 'You have heard from Me; "for John truly baptized with water, but you shall be baptized with the Holy Spirit not many days from now." Acts 1:4-5   Among these disciples were: Peter, Mary the mother of Jesus, John, Matthew, Luke, Mary Magdalene, Bartholomew, James the brother of John, Simon the Canaanite, Jude Thaddaeus, Philip etc. These Believers had seen Jesus Christ do great miracles.

They were most likely there when the Lord healed the blind man, in the Gospel of John, Chapter Nine, this

The Holy Spirit; the Third Person of the Godhead

man's healing caused a stir among the religious leaders of that time; the Pharisees and the Sadducees, they could not find any logical reason for that man receiving his sight, after Jesus had prayed for him. "They brought him who formerly was blind to the Pharisees. Now it was a Sabbath when Jesus made the clay and opened his eyes. Then the Pharisees also asked Him again how he had received his sight. He said to them, "He put clay on my eyes and I washed, and I see." John 9:13-15

The Ministry of our Lord and Savior Jesus Christ when He was here physically on earth was filled with miracles, wonders and signs. Those believers of that time were graced to be part of it.

They Saw the Resurrection of Lazarus from the Dead

Most of these disciples were there at Bethany whereby a man by the name of Lazarus had died and his body was placed in a tomb, and a stone was rolled over the entrance of this man's tomb. His body was already four days in the tomb, when Jesus arrived at Martha and Mary's house where their brother, the deceased, used to live. They witnessed a glorious moment when Jesus

Knowing the Holy Spirit: The Pathway to God's Power

Christ the Son of the Living God, called the dead man by his name, to come out of the tomb! "Now when he had said these things. He cried with a loud voice, "Lazarus come forth!" And he who had died came out bound hand and foot with grave-clothes, and his face was wrapped, with a cloth. Jesus said to them, "Loose him, and let him go." John 11:43-44

They saw that miracle; these disciples had been in Jesus Christ's divine seminary; college; university; institute; school of ministry; etc. I mean, they were trained by the greatest teachers of all time, Jesus Christ himself. In spite of all that, what is astonishing: in the book of Acts, Chapter One, He commanded them not to depart from Jerusalem until they receive the promise from God the Father, the Holy Spirit, the third person of the Godhead. He insisted that for them to be effective and stay focused on sound doctrine of the Kingdom of God, they had to have another teacher who proceeds from God the Father and the Son – the Holy Spirit.

The same Jesus Christ who had commissioned them to go and preach the gospel to all creation and to the uttermost ends of the earth, "And Jesus came and Spoke

The Holy Spirit; the Third Person of the Godhead

To them, saying, "All authority has been given to Me in heaven and on earth. "Go therefore and make disciples of all the nations, baptizing them in the name of the Father and of the Son and of the Holy Spirit, "teaching them to observe all things that I have commanded you; and lo, I am with you always, even to the end of the age." Amen John 28:18-20, He put the whole mission on hold. He literally said don't go out to preach about the Kingdom of God, without the Holy Spirit upon you. Beloved, we need to know Him. They had to experience the presence of the third person of the Godhead, He was to reveal Himself to them in ways they have never experienced before, and that is what is happening to you right now, through these pages of this book illuminated with revelation knowledge from God.

Many of them were on the Mountainside when He was teaching

Many of these disciples were part of the crowd on the mountainside when Jesus was teaching. They had heard amazing words of the Kingdom of God, right from the mouth of Jesus Christ. He was not like any other teachers nor drew from them. Jesus taught with authority, not like any scribe or Rabbi. He said words to them that have never been communicated to that level, to human kind before; words of life and hope. His words produced faith in individuals, which caused them to walk out of diseases, illnesses, bondage, as in the case of a woman who was bent over. "Now He was teaching in one of the synagogues on the Sabbath. And behold, there was a woman who had a spirit of infirmity eighteen years, and was bent over and could in no way raise herself up. But when Jesus saw her, He called her to Him and said to her, "Woman you are loosed from your infirmity." And He laid His hands on her and immediately she was made straight, and glorified God." Luke 13:10-13

Jesus Christ freed this woman supernaturally from her bondage. The word of God had gone forth that day, the disciples were in the synagogue, they leant so much about the kingdom of God. But still Jesus Christ still said to them not to go out to minister, without the Holy Spirit having come upon them. You and I, need to be empowered by God in order to do the will of God. Beloved, we have to know the person of the Holy Spirit.

The Holy Spirit; the Third Person of the Godhead

The Holy Spirit

There has never been any teacher, Rabbi, pastor, prophet, evangelist, apostle, or leader, like Jesus Christ. Those who were part of His earthly ministry when He was here on earth, were privileged to experience a power and revelation knowledge filled ministry; a ministry that had proven heavenly signs and wonders confirming His word, like when He taught in the synagogue in Capernaum, i.e. in the book of St. Mark, Chapter One, from verse twenty-one, to twenty-two, "Then they went into Capernaum, and immediately on the Sabbath He entered the synagogue and taught. And they were astonished at His teaching; for He taught them as one having authority and not as the Scribes." Mark 1: 21-22

Precious one, Bishop Leonard Kayiwa is a Scribe; I do write what the Holy Spirit gives me to write. In the books I write, Jesus is the Lord, I am an under shepherd; He is the Shepherd. All of the preachers and ministers of God that have graced your way, whom we thank God for; they are just messengers – the message is Jesus Christ, and the only one who can keep us all focused and grounded on the sound doctrine of our risen Lord and savior, is the Third Person of the Godhead, the Holy Spirit. All the relentless struggle people find themselves in regard to the interpretation of the Word of God, would be easily resolved if they can simply submit to the leading of the Holy Spirit. I have run into a number of religious groups, who do not even know whether a human being has a spirit. They say, once you die, that is the end of you. Well, I don't want to be part of that religion where I can't go to Heaven, straight away! Like you, I want the best of everything. Others say that there are many ways that lead to God. It is some sort of universalism, but that is not what the Bible teaches. They claim to pray as well as reach God through so many channels and names and their approach is very confusing and powerless, it is a myth; Just because they reject the help of the Holy Spirit: there is only one way – Jesus Christ. "Jesus said to him, "I am the way, the truth and the life. No one comes to the Father except through Me." John 14:6

Pray to God only in the Name of Jesus Christ

In my young days, where I was part of the Catholic faith, the Priests would tell us to pray to God through the names of the apostles; saint Jude, saint Peter, saint John, saint Luke......etc. and Mary, the earthly mother

The Holy Spirit; the Third Person of the Godhead

of Jesus, they would argue and say that these saints were close friends of Jesus Christ and for that reason, if you pray to God through their names, you will get quick attention and receive help in time of need. I saw adults, youth; people of all sorts trying their best to get help through those individual saints who had already passed away! The problem with this scenario, the spirits of those people are not omnipresent, it is only God who is everywhere at the same time, so you can't have people talking to St. Jude everywhere on the earth. That teaching is erroneous, it is not Bible based, but a product of superstitions and traditions of men: we really need to know the Holy Spirit. We need His help.

Those are the unnecessary errors that Jesus Christ, the Second Person of the Godhead, never wanted us to be entangled in, for He loves us. It is only Jesus who died for us on Calvary, not Peter, not John, not Paul, not Mary, not Jude, not Luke, etc. *"Greater love has no one than this, than to lay down one's life for his friends. "You are My friends if you do whatever I command you. "No longer do I call you servants, for a servant does not know what his master is doing; but I have called you friends, for all things that I heard from My Father I have made known to you." John 15:13-15*

Knowing the Holy Spirit: The Pathway to God's Power

The Disciples were there when He Cast Out of a Man an Unclean Spirit in the book of Luke Chapter One from verse twenty-three to verse twenty-eight. They learned something very important in extraordinary circumstances: that evil spirits do exist and they can take abode in human beings, but the good news is, they can be cast out in the Name of Jesus Christ.

These disciples to whom Jesus gave a command after he had been glorified; that is when He had risen from the dead, not depart from Jerusalem, but wait for the promise of the Father Which He said, 'You have heard from me for John truly baptized with water, but you shall be baptized with the Holy Spirit not many days from now'; they were present on that day when Jesus Christ, the Son of the Living God rebuked the unclean spirit, that interrupted, when He was teaching. "Now there was a man in their synagogue with an unclean spirit. And he cried out. Saying, "Let us alone! What have we to do with you, Jesus of Nazareth? Did you come to destroy us? I know who you are – the Holy One of God!" Mark 1:23-24

The disciples of Jesus Christ were very, very highly

The Holy Spirit: the Third Person of the Godhead

trained in the things regarding the Kingdom of God and saw as well as heard for themselves the pleadings of the demonic spirits when they came in contact with the Holy Presence of our Lord Jesus Christ. If any one could argue and say, 'We do not need to wait, we already have had enough training from our divine teacher – Jesus Christ' it would be them, but the teacher; Jesus Christ Himself, said: they had to be baptized with the Holy Spirit and power in order to be His witnesses to the whole world. We have to know the third person of the God Head – the Holy Spirit.

We have sat under many teachers

Precious one reading this anointed script know that You and I, have sat under so many teachers and among those teachers are our parents, who helped us to rise up from crawling to walking. Parents taught us how to speak, they introduced us to good manners; they are the first teachers God gave to us all. Many of them communicated the best information they knew then, to the best of their knowledge, thanks to God for the nice parents, especially those who were God-fearing, God honoring, worshipers of God Almighty, and God lovers with an understanding that evil exists; and that it is necessary to present the young ones for protection to the Lord God Almighty through Jesus Christ, the Savior.

My parents were of the Catholic Religion, so they took me up early in life and had me baptized in the Catholic Church, when I was a baby: that is what they knew then and they were seeking my safety, and devotion to God. You who are reading this book might have been introduced to some other religion. You know you did not choose that religion. It was just handed to you right from the baby stage of life. You went ahead and discovered what it was called later: Catholic faith; Methodist faith; Islam faith; Buddhism; Mormonism; Jehovah Witness; Orthodox; Presbyterian; Judaism, etc., the list goes on and on. We never chose this parents! We happened to find them here and their bliefs.

What I encountered concerning faith while studying in China

I lived in China for a number of years, I was at the university in Nanjing, studying irrigation and Water Conservation Engineering; I do speak Chinese. I studied that language at, the Beijing University of

The Holy Spirit; the Third Person of the Godhead

Languages, in China. I graduated and joined Hahai University where I studied Engineering. I spoke Chinese and wrote in Chinese. I wrote those characters-letters. I would express myself effectively in the Chinese Language, it was taught to me by very highly qualified Chinese professors. However, there is something astonishing that I ran into. When I held friendly conversations with them, as well as with my fellow Chinese students, many of them were told that there was no God, and anything to do with Jesus Christ was just a myth! They would simply say to me; we don't belong to any faith. By that time, I had already received Jesus Christ as my personal savior, I was a 'Born Again Christian,' a Believer.

I knew that God was real; but my friends needed an anointed Born Again, word of God based, Jesus centered, true preacher to tell them the truth, for they were introduced in their upbringing to vanity; they needed to call on the Name of the Lord, "How then shall they call on Him in whom they have not believed?. And how shall they hear without a preacher? And, how shall they preach unless they are sent? As it is written: "How beautiful are the feet of those who preach the Gospel of Peace." Who bring glad tidings of good things!" Rom 10:14-15

I Witness to a Chinese Student and He Becomes a Born Again Christian

My fellow students – the Chinese, were very smart, intelligent, and they worked hard on their day-to-day class assignments. We all studied hard and did our best, but the fact that they did not know the resurrected Lord; Jesus Christ as their Lord and Personal Savior, bothered me.

I started preaching to some who came close to me. There was on particular case that produced good fruits, it was a Chinese student who was studying in a university that trained students to handle and learn international languages, especially English, Russian, Korean, German and Swahili. This university was in Nanjing, not very far away from my university. This particular Chinese student became very interested in what I had to say about God. Something else that caught his attention was when he saw my grade scores in the School of Engineering. He thought I was genius. Well, I gave him an English Bible and encouraged him to read the New Testament. He would come to me with

The Holy Spirit; the Third Person of the Godhead

many questions, and I tried my best through the help of the Holy Spirit, to answer them as well as to explain to him the scriptures. Something else which he benefited from when he came around me, was an opportunity to practice the English language, for he was majoring in English and Russian. This young man became 'Born Again.' He received Jesus Christ as his Lord and personal savior. I totally believe that for this conversion to take place, it was a result of my being Baptized in the Holy Spirit, the Third Person of the Godhead. He helped me to help this Chinese friend of mine —who became a child of God.

It is not necessarily how you start, or where you start, you can be in a mess right now concerning what you believe, but thanks to God, help has come your way. This book in your hand is part of that help, possibly you were told that you do not need the Holy Spirit! Well, in this book you are going to find out that God, the Holy Spirit is that one you would want to be in agreement with and to know. That will make your finish in life glorious, meaningful and worth it all.

You and I, we are now together on this trip, amidst very sound teaching from the Lord, God Almighty. In case you are not yet 'Born Again' it is time for you to give your life to our Lord and Savior Jesus Christ, for

Knowing the Holy Spirit: The Pathway to God's Power

Jesus Christ said, in the Gospel of John Chapter Three, verse three, "Jesus answered and said to him, "Most assuredly, I say to you, unless one is born again, he cannot see the kingdom of God." John 3:3

You need to see the Kingdom of God, that is why you are in possession of this book, for the Kingdom of God is not just in words; it is not powerless religions. The Kingdom of Heaven is in Christ Jesus and it is of power. The Holy Spirit does reveal it to us. "For the Kingdom of God is not in word but in power." 1 Cor 4:20. You need the power of God in your life. So Confess Christ as Lord and Savior into your life, invite him in your heart, "that if you confess with your mouth the Lord Jesus and believe in your heart that God has raised Him from the dead, you will be saved. For with the heart one believes unto righteousness, and with the mouth Confession is made unto Salvation." Rom 10:9-10

In case you have done that; received Jesus as your personal savior; you are now a 'Born Again' Believer, you are a true Christian. The word 'Christian', has a word Christ in it; which means, Anointed One. The Implication is that; you are part of the anointed One; you are Christ like: You can be empowered by the Holy Spirit, the Third Person of the Godhead, to live a victor-

The Holy Spirit; the Third Person of the Godhead

ius, fruitful life. A life that is not self-centered but God centered. Find a Jesus Christ Centered Church, a Church that is Bible based, were Jesus Christ is Lord and Savior, and the Holy Spirit of God is welcome.

Saint Paul asks the Believers at Ephesus, 'Did you receive the Holy Spirit, when you believed?'

Apostle Paul wrote a number of Bible Books in the new testament: He wrote the book of Romans, 1 Corinthians, 2 Corinthians, Galatians, Ephesians, Philippians, Colossians, etc. This man, to him, God revealed the richness of the Kingdom of God. He flowed in revelation knowledge. He was an amazing teacher of the Word of God; his teachings through the Holy Spirit have blessed numerous people around the world. It is through his writings in the Epistles, that we understand, that we are saved by grace through faith, "For by grace you have been saved through faith, and that not of yourselves; it is the gift of God, not of works, lest anyone should boast. For we are His workmanship, created in Christ Jesus for good works, which God prepared beforehand that we should walk in them." Eph 2:8-10

That scripture is profound, in a nutshell, our identity is mapped out as well as what we became when we received Jesus Christ as our Lord and Savior. That kind

Knowing the Holy Spirit: The Pathway to God's Power

of knowledge, that Paul penned down, could not have been from his human intelligence. We all know that when He relied on his intellectual power, before his conversion to Christianity, he messed up everything. He was a mess and a plague, instead of being a blessing, he persecuted the people who believed the things he later had to live by – the Holy Word of God. This man knew what it was like to live far below the grace of our Lord Jesus Christ, he had lived a religious life, whereby he was royal to creeds, rituals and religious ceremonies: he tried his best to serve God outside submission to the Lord Jesus Christ and it did not work very well for him. He had turned into a hateful, bitter, vile, none tolerant, violent person. "Then Saul, still breathing threats and murder against the disciples of the Lord, went to the high priest and asked letters from him to the synagogues of Damascus, so that if he found any who were of the Way, whether men or women, he might bring them bound to Jerusalem." Acts 9:1-2.

Saul's religious persuasion never turned him into a peaceful person, but the opposite. There are people today under the same spell that Paul was operating under before conversion, all they have is empty religion; no power, no heavenly wisdom; no peace and no regard for other people; it is all about them: 'me, me,

The Holy Spirit; the Third Person of the Godhead

me' and 'mine.' It took divine intervention from our Lord Jesus Christ to set Paul who formerly was called Saul on the right course, and without the help from the Third Person of the Godhead – the Holy Spirit, Paul would have vanished in history as a sounding brass or a clanging cymbal. *"Though I speak with the tongues of men and of angels, but have not love, I have become as sounding brass or a clanging cymbal." I Cor 13:1* Are you surprised that when he came to Ephesus on his missionary journey and found believers there-that is disciples of our Lord Jesus Christ, *"he said to them, "Did you receive the Holy Spirit when you believed?" So they said to him, "We have not so much as heard whether there is a Holy Spirit." Acts 19:2,* Your situation might be similar to that of these disciples, for I know this book will find its way into the hands of all sorts of people. The good news is you are in the right university at the opportune time. This is part of the inspired resources that God in His omniscience foreordained for you. On the day you were born, you enrolled in the University of Life, with a potential to enroll in the Divine University of the Holy Spirit. In the University of Life, you learned that without Jesus Christ, you can do nothing. You cannot even chase away one little demon nor can you create your own

Knowing the Holy Spirit: The Pathway to God's Power

Heaven. You don't know who even you are, really, nor do you understand what befalls you. Sometimes, what is good in your eyes, is just disaster. These disciples did not know whether there was a Holy Spirit, they needed someone anointed to help them, and in this case, it was Paul. Please stay with me on this glorious voyage, we will both arrive to a productive conclusion – we need the Holy Spirit of God!!!

The Apostle Paul laid his hands on them and they did receive the Holy Spirit. "And when Paul had laid hands on them, the Holy Spirit came upon them, and they spoke with tongues and prophesied. Now the men were about twelve in all." Acts 19:6 Beloved we need to know the Holy Spirit, the Third person of the Godhead; the Holy Spirit is the pathway to God's power.

The Holy Spirit Guides Us into the Whole Truth

Paul knew that these precious believers needed someone bigger than a human being or an angel or an institution, to help them walk as well as enjoy the Christ like life they had received.

These believers were not just designated to be members of a church; they were supposed to be disciples of our Lord Jesus Christ. Those who can dare do the works of God. As according to the words of the

The Holy Spirit; the Third Person of the Godhead

Lord in the book of John, Chapter Fourteen, verse twelve, "Most assuredly I say to you, he who believes in Me, the works that I do he will do also; and greater works than these he will do because I go to my Father," John 14:12

Jesus had said to His disciples that it was good for us that He returns to His Father, for then the Helper will come. One who will help us see the things of God as well as receive the free gift of salvation. "Nevertheless, I tell you the truth. It is to your advantage that I go away, for if I do not go away, the Helper will not come to you: but if I depart, I will send Him to you. "And when He has come, He will convict the world of sin, and of righteousness, and of judgment." John 16:7-8. We need to know the Holy Spirit.

The Holy Spirit is not some human prophet. There are teachings out there, especially in the Moslem religion whereby their teachers tell their followers that the one that Jesus Christ referred to in John 16:7 was a man called Mohammed of the Islamic Faith. Please, whoever is reading this book; God is leading me to lay it out to you very clearly, that Jesus Christ was not referring at all to the man depicted as 'Prophet Mohammed of the Moslem faith.' Mohamed died long ago, never rose from the dead. He is nowhere mentioned in the Holy Bible. This man was a human being, with a human spirit. Those professors, teachers, Imams, Sheikhs, and religious leaders, need this book very urgently, they need to become born again. They need the Holy Spirit in order to say the right things about God. "For what Man Knows the things of a man except the spirit of the man which is in him? Even so, no one knows the things of God except the Spirit of God." 1Cor 2:11 The Holy Spirit is from God and is God. Any religion that claims knowledge of God without acknowledging the deity of the Holy Spirit, you don't need to follow, nor to be part of. Any human being claiming to be a prophet or a messenger of God, even if it is an angel, that does not acknowledge that Jesus Christ is the Son of the Living God, as well as the Lamb of God, that was sacrificed for our atonement of sin, is not a true messenger of God, but one with a false message. In case you have been misled, through erroneous teachings, please just abandon those teachings. God loves you.

Powerlessness and Confusion of Mind is not at all God's Will for You and the Church

You cannot afford to be spiritually weak on earth. There is so much going on in the spiritual realm. Psychics are very active in big cities as well as villages

The Holy Spirit; the Third Person of the Godhead

Sorcery is aired on T.V. channels, radio, and social media; demons are on the loose, causing drug epidemics, violence in homes and at places of work. Hate crimes have escalated. Certain behaviors that are contrary to God's word, are being celebrated by certain groups, devils are indirectly asking for rights in the Supreme Courts around the world.

That alone requires that we have a helper, one who is not limited; one who is not a creation, but one who is part of the God Head. One who is omnipresent and omniscient, as well as omnipotent: One who proceed from God the Father and God the Son, and in whom there is no inconsistency. This one is none other than the blessed third person of the Godhead – The Holy Spirit.

EL-SHADDAI

GOD

ALMIGHTY

2

THE

HOLY SPIRIT

IS NOT AN IT

Has a personality

"Can two walk together unless they are agreed?" Amos 3:3

Sometime ago, that is in the year of our Lord 1975, I happened to attend a service in a big cathedral, in one of the cities of Uganda called Masaka. I was then a student at St. Henry's College, Kitovu. This particular day was referred to as the Day of Pentecost. This very big denomination does celebrate that day throughout their churches, all over the world. The place was packed, people even stood outside in big numbers, a very renown Bishop in that region was the one that presided over that Mass. This man entered the pulpit

The Holy Spirit; the Third Person of the Godhead

and motioned to everyone to be quiet, for he was going to teach as well as explain what the Holy Spirit is. I was then in my early teen years, attending school at the College and very interested in learning something new. The whole place was quiet; you could hear a pin drop, it seemed like we were very anxious, desiring to know who the Holy Spirit really is.

This Bishop of that big denomination was renowned scholar in their seminaries and universities. He had a lot of doctorate degrees and many took seriously what he taught. There were a lot of Priests in attendance that day, as well as seminary students. So, whatever was going to be said, would impact a big number of people.

The Man Erroneously Describes the Holy Spirit as an It- a Force

This man taught and said that the Holy Spirit is some sort of a power or force that proceeds from God the Father and the Son; he pushed further the theory that it is that thing that God the Father uses to get things done here on earth. I noticed that as he taught, he never gave us any scriptures from the Holy Bible as reference to his

The Holy Spirit is Not an It: He has a Personality

theory, in fact in that denomination, during those days, Christians were never allowed to have Bibles nor to bring them to their church services. We only depended on what those priests told us. I was puzzled at his teachings because in the same sermon he referred to the Holy Spirit as the Third Person of the Godhead, having all the attributes of God!

How I Analyzed His Sermon as a Student

At school, I was studying mathematics, physics, biology, chemistry, geography, history, English, technical drawing, agriculture, accounts. As academicians, words meant something to us. We were taught to distinguish between that which is a "it" from that which is a living organism. We analyzed forces and elements, we learned characteristics of specimen; we would study the characteristics of animals, birds, reptiles and properly distinguish them from one another.

We knew what electricity was; what water was; what air was; what metals were...etc., and could clearly present their physical and chemical characteristics.

The preacher that day, went on to describe the Holy

The Holy Spirit; the Third Person of the Godhead

Spirit as something like electricity, that goes forth and causes things to happen. I, being a very attentive and curious student as well as my fellow students who were there, were not satisfied at his description of the Third Person of the Godhead – The Holy Spirit. We thought something was very, very wrong with that analysis. We talked about it among ourselves, but we lacked a book to look at in order to find the truth, for we were never introduced to the Holy Bible by that denomination. We never owned Bibles, nor were we encouraged to read them.

There was obviously confusion in regard to that teaching, the audience was confused and the Bishop seemed to be struggling in the process of advancing that teaching. He seemed to have been presenting to people what was handed over to him in the seminary and that which was taught worldwide in that denomination. There is a scripture in the Holy Bible, in the Book of First Corinthians, Chapter Fourteen, verse thirty-three: "For God is not the author of confusion but of peace, as in all the churches of the Saints." I Cor 14:33

The Holy Spirit is not an It: Has a Personality

You and I, we have the same concern here, regarding that erroneous teaching; why should a force or some type of power be called God? We all kind of know that God is not an it: God talks; God hears; God reasons; God can laugh; God can be grieved; God loves; God can see, and is a creator, not a creation.

Well, in that service that day, no one was healed, delivered or filled with the Holy Spirit. There was no tangible presence of the power of God, the only thing we walked away with was confusion and uncertainty in regard to the person of the Third Person of the Godhead, the Holy Spirit.

Why It Is Important to Know the Person of the Holy Spirit

The opening scripture of this chapter is, "Can two walk together Unless they are agreed?" Amos 3:3 As I am writing this book, I am a married husband with a wife. There are so many things we do together, as a married couple, in fact, it is so beautiful for us as pastors to function in unity. I did not marry an it!! My wife is a person; she has feelings. She loves the things of God.

The Holy Spirit; the Third Person of the Godhead

She loves people, she sings in the church; she is a worship leader, she preaches as well as teaches the word of God. My wife has all the attributes of a living human being; she can be made happy and can also be grieved, she is not an it, for that reason I can't treat her the same way I treat electricity or water or a vehicle, nor an animal. She has the nature of God in her life, "Then God said, "Let us make man in Our image, according to Our likeness, let them have dominion over the fish of the sea, over the birds of the air; and over the cattle over all the earth and over every creeping thing that creeps on the earth." Gen 1:26

That scripture itself is very revealing, about the nature of God; from that verse we do conclude that God has to be able to speak, feel, hear, love, laugh, bless…etc. Our personality as human beings was drawn out of the likeness of God; we speak because God speaks, we hear because God hears, we love for God loves as well, we fellowship because there is fellowship in the Godhead. We are creative, because God is a creator. Beloved, it is time to abandon anything which is not God-like, and aggressively receive the Word of God in regard to the person of the Holy Spirit.

The Holy Spirit is Not an it; Has a Personality

Agreement is a "must" for a relationship to work

The concept of agreement is universal; for any community, group, people, nation, place of work, to function in harmony, there has to be agreement. There has to be principals, norms, concepts and rules that are agreed upon. Agreement is birthed out of good understanding and knowledge, for people are destroyed for lack of knowledge, "My people are destroyed for lack of knowledge. Because you have rejected knowledge, I also will reject you from being priest for me. Because you have forgotten the law of your God, I also will forget your children." Hos 4:6

You would have a lot of accidents right here in the U.S.A. in the year of our Lord 2018, the year that I am writing this book; if people did not agree to stop at the red light, if some would say, 'No, rules don't matter, you just keep on driving.' I want to assure you that many would be maimed, and some dead at just failing to come in agreement with the concept of stopping at the red light. This also applies to stop signs, someone has to be able to yield to the other, as well as come to a

The Holy Spirit; the Third Person of the Godhead

complete stop. I recall, when I first arrived in the United States of America, I was then living in Tulsa, Oklahoma, and I needed a United States driving license. I went down to the Secretary of State office to obtain one. Well, they decided to have me take an exam as well as a driving test. I knew that I was a very good driver and having grown up around a specialist in automobile engineering, the brother of my mother, I had spent a lot of time during school holidays in his automobile workshop, learning how to fix cars as well as driving them around. I was really confident that I had good command of a vehicle. I also learned driving by operating the family tractor, a 744 International when I was about 14 years of age. I would drive it while pulling a trailer, I could even dig with it.

My upbringing was very industrious. Throughout all of the school holidays, I had to be working in the family business. My father was a businessman who owned a lot of land, some trucks, some boats, factories, a tractor, a cattle ranch, a farm, fishing site, etc. We, the children, were very actively involved in all of those activities,

The Holy Spirit is Not an It: Has a Personality

as well as going to school and studying hard. That is why I am able to write this book, in a language that I learned at school. Beloved, you having this book in your hand, is proof that you are willing to walk with the Holy Spirit and be blessed.

The day came for me to take my driving test, a police officer entered my car and asked me to drive to a certain location. Well, I said that was good, I am going to do my best. I drove, stopped at the lights, put on the indicators when turning, observed all the speed limits, there was also a stop sign on my way, that I thought I had handled well and I really thought that I had to get my driver's license that day. But, to my surprise, when we returned to the office, the police officer said, 'You did not come to a full stop when you came to a stop sign, therefore; you have to take the test again.' I said, 'I stopped a little bit!' He said to me, 'You don't stop a little bit, you come to a full stop.!' Beloved, I had to come in agreement with the rules that govern driving in the U.S.A. in order for me to get the driving license. So it is with the Holy Spirit, the Third Person of the Godhead. You have to come in total Agreement with

The Holy Spirit; the Third person of the Godhead

Him, according to the Word of God concerning the Holy Spirit. We all need to know the Word of God, to read it, as well as meditate on it. Regarding my driver's license, I took the test again, came to a complete stop at the stop sign, and guess what! I obtained an American driver's license that day.

As a Bishop, I conduct weddings, and if you are familiar with this ceremony, one of the first opening statements is: 'Do you agree to take so and so as your lawfully wedded husband, or wife.' If any of the would be married couples say, 'No.' we cannot proceed any further, to make it plain, that union is not necessary, for they are not in agreement.

You can have all the papers and qualifications to do a certain job, but when you go to the place of employment and disagree with their rules: those people might find themselves in an awkward position whereby they have to let you go, for you are not in agreement with them.

Major wars have been fought out of disagreements. Countries have battled over border boundaries, one

The Holy Spirit is Not an It: Has a Personality

group of people says, that piece of land is ours; the other says, no, it is ours, the next thing, war breaks out and people end up losing their lives. We have seen this situation in regard to the former Soviet Union countries and territories, North Korea vs South Korea. I saw that during the dictatorship, in Uganda between 1971 and 1972, when they annexed part of the land that belong to the nation of Tanzania, causing a war that ousted the dictator and his thugs, resulting in the death of a lot of people. This also happened during the First World War and the Second World War by a crazy dictatorship in Germany. Precious one, for two to walk together, they have to agree, and you can't agree with what you don't understand. That is why we need to know who the Third Person of the Godhead, the Holy Spirit, is.

When Two Agree

There is a very powerful scripture about the power of being in agreement, a word given to human beings by the Second Person of the Godhead – Jesus Christ. "Again I say to you that if two of you agree on earth concerning anything that they ask, it will be done for them by My Father in heaven. "For where two or three are gathered together in My name, I am there in the

The Holy Spirit; the Third Person of the Godhead

midst of them." Matt 18:19-20   This scripture makes the point of agreement so important, especially that God Almighty promises to honor the prayers of His people. Gracious one, we all need our prayers answered, especially in things in regard to our day to day living, we want to support our families, we desire our children to be safe at home and at school, we want peace in our communities; not violence. It is our prayers to have more cures of diseases discovered so that we live healthy, long lives – the list goes on and on. The good news is God promises to answer our petitions if we will come in agreement with His word and ourselves. Someone has to come in agreement with somebody.

You Have to Know the Likes of Someone in Order for You to Adequately Agree with Them

In a relationship, one has to have knowledge of the other partner's interest, that partner could be a spouse, relative, person at work, a parent or a friend. The people who first took care of all of us were our parents, these two persons have us when we are so fragile, at the time when we need all of their help in order for us to live. It was a time when we were so vulnerable to so many challenges. When we are born to these parents,

The Holy Spirit is Not an It: He Has a Personality

Almost at all times, we tend to participate in what they value, whether it is music, food, people they associate with, or places they go to. These parents of ours know what we do not know, and God put it in their hearts to share what they know and what they have with us – I am talking about reasonable parents.

One of the things you discover as you grow in the family environment are the likes and the dislikes of your parents. Many parents desire that their children become people with good morals, someone respectful, one they could caution about some dangerous things, and they could heed to their advice. They mean good for you, and they understand that you being young, many times you act as a child. "When I was a child, I spoke as a child, I understood as a child, I thought as a child, but when I became a man, I put away childish things." I Cor 13:11

The Role of Parents in our Upbringing

Our parents understood that we were children and did all that they knew how to help us develop to adulthood. They also prayed to God that we would honor their counsel, for our good. "For "He who would

The Holy Spirit; the Third Person of the Godhead

love life and good days. Let him refrain his tongue from evil. And his lips from speaking deceit. Let him turn away from evil and do good; Let him seek peace and pursue it. For the eyes of the LORD are on the righteous, And His ears are open to their prayers; But the face of the LORD is against those who do evil." 1 Pet 3:10-12 Most reasonable parents would like their children to have good success in life, and this works very well, as children understand that their parents are not an it, but one with feelings and concerns as themselves.

The Holy Spirit Can Be Grieved

The Holy Spirit has feelings and can respond to the way we treat Jesus Christ, as well as the way we treat other people, as well as to the decisions we make in life. Paul understood this very well, especially that God did unusual miracles through his life. "Now God worked unusual miracles by the hands of Paul. So that even handkerchiefs or aprons were brought from his body to the sick, and the diseases left them and the evil spirts went out of them." Acts 19:11-12 Paul had received

The Holy Spirit is Not an It: Has a Personality

 Power when the Holy Spirit came upon him, and he was a witness to so many people; he was a soul winner like you and I, I mean somebody willing to lift Jesus Christ on earth so that many turn to righteousness.

This beloved Paul, walked with the Holy Spirit of God and had some understanding of the likes and the dislikes of the Third Person of the Godhead, he did not see the Holy Spirit as an 'It'. In his writings in the book of Ephesians the fourth chapter, verse thirty to thirty-two; this is what we are given as the Body of Christ. "And do not grieve the Holy Spirit of God, by whom you were sealed for the day of redemption. Let all bitterness, wrath, anger, clamor, and evil speaking be put away from you, with malice. And be kind to one another, tenderhearted, forgiving one another, even as God in Christ forgave you." Eph 4:30-32

It is the Holy Spirit that Manifests the Power of God. You don't want to Grieve Him

In the book of Judges, we have the story of Samson, this man was separated to being a Nazirite, from the time he was conceived in the womb of his mother. Instructions were also given to her parents by God Almighty through an Angel of God, concerning how to raise up that child. "And the Angel of the LORD

The Holy Spirit; the Third Person of the Godhead

appeared to the woman and said to her. "Indeed now you are barren and have borne no children, but you shall conceive and bear a son. "Now therefore please be careful not to drink wine or similar drinks, and not to eat anything unclean. "For behold you shall conceive and bear a son. And no razor shall come upon his head, for the child shall be a Nazirite to God from the womb: and he shall begin to deliver Israel out of the hands of the Philistines." Jud 13:3-5

Samson was set apart by God's predetermined counsel, to operate in amazing supernatural power in order to help the Children of Israel come out of the bondage and oppression of the Philistines. The Third Person of the Godhead; the Holy Spirit, empowered him to do unusual things in the process of his obedience to carry out the divine commission on his life like this, "When he came to Lehi, the Philistines came shouting against him. Then the Spirit of the LORD; came mightily upon him; and the ropes that were on his arms became like flax that is burned with fire, and his bonds broke loose from his hands. He found a fresh jaw bone

The Holy Spirit is Not an It: Has a Personality

of a donkey, reached out his hands and took it, and killed a thousand men with it." Jud 15:14-15 Even himself was overwhelmed at what had happened through his life. In the natural strength of a man that could not happen. For first of all, he was bound with fresh ropes, and his assailants were armed to the teeth, as well as outnumbered him. Samson himself in the following verse expresses the surprise of this miracle. "Then Samson said: with the jaw bone of the donkey, Heaps upon Heaps, with the Jaw bone of a donkey I have slain a thousand men!" Jud 15:16

We, also are set apart like Samson

When you received Jesus Christ as your personal Savior you became a new creature, according to Second Corinthians chapter Five, Verse Seventeen, "Therefore, if anyone is in Christ, he is a new creation: old things are passed away; behold, all things have become new." 2 Cor 5:17 We are now children of the Kingdom of God. We are no longer mere men or mere women. We are a royal priesthood, peculiar. Our bodies are the temple of the Holy Spirit; God is right with us as well

The Holy Spirit; the Third Person of the Godhead

As in us, "Or do you not know that your body is the temple of the Holy Spirit who is in you. Whom you have from God and you are not your own." I Cor 6:19 This scripture brings it out strongly that we are not walking alone, but with the Third Person of the Godhead – the Holy Spirit. Child of God, we should avoid grieving the Holy Spirit; that might be the reason why we don't see tangible power of God in a number of places of worship, as well as in the lives of many people.

We have been given the Great Commission of making Disciples of all nations, Baptizing them in the Name of the Father, the Son and the Holy Spirit. And teaching them to observe all things that have been handed over to us through the Word of God in the Holy Bible. We are entrusted with the Gospel, the Good News to the world: that is; Jesus came in flesh, was born by a virgin woman, Mary, suffered through the hands of sinful men, was crucified on the cross for our sins, died and rose from the dead after three days, for our justification. That Jesus is alive and well and does save, deliver, set free, as well as makes lives new. In addition, heaven is real.

The Holy Spirit is Not an It: Has a Personality

Our mission is so powerful that it enables human beings to decide where they are going to spend eternity. Either in Heaven, or in Hell. Signs and wonders are supposed to follow us; we are destined to be people of power through the Holy Spirit's presence in our lives.

What causes one to be grieved.

In the natural, when somebody or something does not do what is supposed to be done or when somebody does not cooperate with the laid out rules, even when everything has been clearly laid out for their benefit, as well as for the benefit of others; that can lead to one who loves you to be grieved. The implication here is, when someone, especially knows the consequences of your refusal to obey the set rules, or your failure to carry out the laid down instructions for your benefit.

There are situations when the help out of the dire situation one is in is available, but one refuses to use it, and someone ends up being hurt. Cases where one is under attack by demonic spirits and the only way to attain freedom is to submit to the Lordship of Jesus Christ, and receive authority from Him over these evil spirits, or to go to those believers who have authority over demons and be prayed for. They have authority

The Holy Spirit; the Third Person of the Godhead

from Jesus Christ, "Behold, I give you the authority, to trample on serpents and scorpions and over all the power of the enemy, and nothing Shall by any means hurt you." Luke 10:19

As a pastor, I have watched people go through Hell, caused by demonic, evil forces; spells due to sorcery, witchcraft, drugs, but for some reason, they are yet to be willing to receive help from the Holy Spirit of God. These kind of acts of rejecting help from God through His word by us human beings, causes the Holy Spirit to be grieved.

Let us learn from Samson's case.

As long as Samson kept the secret of his power to himself, as instructed by God, he continued prevailing over the Philistines; for God the Holy Spirit was there with him to redeem him from the attacks of the Philistines, as well as to break the yolks and bonds they had put over the children of Israel. However, down the road, Samson started getting involved in a number of out of order behaviors; then went further and told the secret of his power. He told them that when they shave his hair, his strength will leave him, and that is exactly what happened. He allowed the enemies of Israel to know his secret and they shaved his hair off his head;

The Holy Spirit is Not an It: Has a Personality

That Grieved the Holy Spirit, by whom he was sealed for the day of redemption. "And do not grieve the Holy Spirit of God, by whom you were sealed for the day of redemption." Eph 4:30 When the Philistines attacked Samson again, there was no manifestation of the power of God, for God had departed from him, and sadly, he did not know that.

"And she said, "The Philistines are upon you Samson, so he awoke from his sleep and said, "I will go out as before, at other times, and shake myself free!" But he did not know that the LORD, had departed from him. Then they took him and put out his eyes. ...." Jud 16: 20-21 This particular example lets us know that when we grieve the Holy Spirit of God, we can end up without the benefits of His presence. My brother, my sister, the Holy Spirit is not an 'it,' He is God; the Third Person of the Godhead, we need Him and we need His help, especially through this turbulent journey of ours on earth.

God Grieved in Gen 6:6

There is another place in the Holy Bible where the word Grieved is applied to God in light of the events that took place then. The Bible says, "Then the LORD saw that the wickedness of man was great in the earth,

The Holy Spirit; the Third Person of the Godhead

And that every intent of the thoughts of his heart was only evil continually." Gen 6:5 The preceding Bible verses reveals to us the tragedy of the sons of God that left their place of abode and decided to take wives from among the daughters of men, and ended up corrupting the human race. Verse nine of Genesis Chapter Six, points out what would have been done by these human beings so that they not fall victim of those other creations, who took advantage of them. The way to stay out of trouble, was to walk with God, and that is exactly what Noah did. "This is the genealogy of Noah. Noah was a Just man, perfect in his generations. Noah walked with God." Gen 6:9 That is what all the other human beings were supposed to do. They were meant to dwell in the secret place of the Most High. "He who dwells in the secret place of the Most High Shall abide under the Shadow of the Almighty." Ps 91:1

Noah was in God's hands: the spirits called, sons of God which transgressed and invaded mankind, to take daughters out of them for themselves, could not touch Noah's family, for he was in the secret place of the Most High. Those other people relied on their natural strength and intelligence. They were not in agreement

The Holy Spirit is Not an It: He has a Personality

With the Holy Spirit of God, they chose their own ways: verse three sheds light on that, "and the LORD said, "My Spirit shall not strive with man forever, for he is indeed flesh; yet his days shall be one hundred and twenty years. Gen 6:3 Before that time human beings lived for a very long time. They would live up to nine hundred years, eight hundred years, seven hundred years, but after that time the years of human beings on earth were reduced to a maximum of around one hundred and twenty years.

The years of man's life on earth were reduced due to grieving God

God can be grieved, that is, when we chose ways that are contrary to His nature and leading, when we don't let Him help us, His way. For the way of the LORD is the best. The consequences of God withdrawing His Spirit pertaining to the longevity of man's life is evident around us, rarely do people live over one hundred and twenty years.

It is very evident in this story that when we grieve God, we may disqualify ourselves from His: protection, power, miracles, wonders, signs, financial provisions,

The Holy Spirit; the Third Person of the Godhead

joy, peace and His presence. One root cause of this is the failure to acknowledge that the Third Person of the God Head is not an it, but has a personality and can be pleased or grieved.

Four Persons: Two Men and Two Ladies Come to Preach to Us an erroneous Gospel

It was morning on that Saturday, we were still at home, me and my dear wife; when I heard a knock on the door. We lived in a neighborhood that had a good amount of privacy. Big homes, very well cared for, in the United States of America. I looked out through the window of our bedroom on the second floor and saw a number of well-dressed men and women going to different houses and knocking on the doors. They even had a badge on their suits and dresses to identify them in regard to the religious group to which they belonged.

I came down the stairs and welcomed them into our house politely, I received them in our living room. They said to me we have come to show you the way of God. Well, I said that is fine, 'What do you have?' They were holding a small book in their hands and

The Holy Spirit is Not an It; Has a Personality

claimed that that book was given to the founder of their religious group by an Angel from God, at that time, my wife joined us as well. Two came in first, then another two came and knocked on the door of our gorgeous home, I gladly welcomed them in as well. I love people.

The little Book

What our guests had was a little book, blue in color and everything they were talking about they based it on that book. They explained that that book was the later Gospel added to the Holy Bible. That alarmed me and my wife. We nearly shouted 'Blasphemy' but we held our peace, for we wanted to be good students and treat our guests with honor! These people wanted to turn us away from the true Gospel we had heard and received, like how they had possibly done to many others already, "I marvel that you are turning away so soon from Him who called you in the grace of Christ, to a different gospel, which is not another; but there are some who trouble you and.. pervert the gospel of Christ "Gal1:6-7

These people had a different gospel, and they referred to themselves as Mormons, as well as The Church of Christ of the Later Days. Please, I am just telling you a historic fact. I am not trying to paint a bad

The Holy Spirit; the Third Person of the Godhead

nasty picture of anyone, always remember, none of us were born with a religion, it was only handed to us by some people, so since we are of age now, we can do something about it, by making the right choices.

I noticed that they were very highly motivated, and wanted to share what they had with every human being on earth, and I being a Bishop, I was very curious about their persuasion, where does it come from? I also wondered if they properly understood God, whom they were talking to us about. I thought, 'Oh, these precious people are trying their best with what they know; they are out seeking for people to convert to their doctrine.'

To these people, the little book they had was more of an authority, to base on their preaching than the Holy Bible! "As we have said before, so now I say again, if anyone preaches any other gospel to you than what you have received, let him be accursed." Gal 1:9 Those precious ladies and gentlemen did not seem to mean anything bad, they were only passing what was handed over to them, they had the wrong book, and ran with that information to win over people to that religion, they did not know any better. They were only members of a religious group, not Disciples Jesus Christ. Stay with me and you will find out for yourself the truth about this

this narrative, from what conspired after some time with them.

I Request Permission to Ask Them About the Holy Spirit

As they continued sharing with us their religion, I lovingly motioned to them to allow us to ask them some questions, which they willingly consented to. My first question was: 'Who is the Holy Spirit?'

One of them said; 'It is a force like electricity proceeding from God.'

The other one said; 'I am not sure what it is, but it is some sort of power, I guess.'

The third one said; 'It is the creative mechanism God uses to get things done. It is not God, but it comes from God.'

The fourth one said; 'I really do not know: it is a very confusing subject for many, we need more teaching about it. Then I asked them to bring a Bible and read to us John 16:13, Amazing enough, without any objection or ill feeling, They went out to their cars and each one

The Holy Spirit; the Third Person of the Godhead

brought a Bible of their version. My wife and I had the New King James Version in our hands. You need to know I am a soul winner, as much as they were interested in turning us to their religion; inside us, we were thanking God for bringing them right into our home, that we may witness to them. This is what they found in the Gospel of John, Chapter Sixteen from verse thirteen to verse fifteen, and this is Jesus Christ himself, the second person of the Godhead speaking:

"However when He, the Spirit of truth has come, He will guide you into all truth; for He will not speak on His own authority but whatever He hears, He will speak: and He will tell you things to come." He will glorify me for He will take of what is mine and declare it to you. 'All things that the Father has are mine, Therefore, I said that He will take of Mine and declare it to you." John 16:13-15

As you are aware of the opening scripture in this chapter is: Can two walk together unless they agree, and for one to treat someone else as a friend, you have to know their person or else you can do things to that particular individual that you would not do if you had

The Holy Spirit is Not an It: Has a Personality

a better understanding of them, especially in the light that they are not an it, but they have a personality, like you do.

Avoiding Striving with The Holy Spirit

"And the LORD said, "My Spirit shall not strive with man forever, for he is indeed flesh; yet his days shall be one hundred and twenty years." Gen 6:3

Those soul winners, who came to our home, became very alarmed when they read the Gospel of John with us in Chapter Sixteen from verse Thirteen to Fifteen. There was a revelation in there that they could not get away from about the Holy Spirit. These are some of the things, they found out about the Third Person of the Godhead, and they are for you as well:

The Holy Spirit can speak -

We all agree that the origin of the Third Person of the Godhead is not from man, it is not man who formed or made the Holy Spirit; The Holy Spirit is a creator, not a creation. We further agree that the one who is very qualified to introduce the Holy Spirit to us, is the Second Person of the Godhead, Jesus Christ. Beloved,

The Holy Spirit; the Third Person of the Godhead

Any religion, group, person or system that tries to define the Third Person of the Godhead outside of Jesus' spectrum, they are bound to error. Those precious visitors of ours did not know that the Holy Spirit can speak!!! They were told by their pastors and teachers, as well as apostles, and prophets in conjunction with their evangelists; to narrow it down, their priests, that the Holy Spirit is a force, some sort of power that comes from God and does not have the ability to communicate. This alone is ground for strife because how will you accept counsel from something you do not believe can even speak to you?

The Holy Spirit Said: -

In the book of Acts, Chapter Thirteen, the disciples at Antioch prayed and fasted; among them were prophets, and teachers as well as apostles. In Verses one to three we notice something worthy of examining very closely, the word, 'The Holy Spirit said' to these precious Believers in the book of Acts, the Holy Spirit was not an it: But one who had a personality and could speak and deliver to them a God counsel. These early believers knew that the Holy Spirit does speak; they

The Holy Spirit is Not an It; Has a Personality

believed that He who created the mouth of a man to speak, is able to talk as well. "As they ministered to the lord and fasted, the Holy Spirit said, "Now separate to Me Barnabas and Saul for the work to which I have called them." Then having fasted and prayed, and laid hands on them, they sent them away. 'So being sent out by the Holy Spirit.........." Acts 13:2-4 This church at Antioch was in agreement with the Holy Spirit.

They were walking with the Third Person of the Godhead out of submission, they were well taught and had good understanding of the Person of the Holy Spirit, that is why a book like this is in your hands today, for God is equipping you for the work of ministry. "And He Himself gave some to be apostles, some prophets, some evangelists, and some pastors and teachers, for the equipping of the saints for the work of ministry, for the edifying of the body of Christ, till we all come to the unity of the faith and of the knowledge of the Son of God, to a perfect man, to the measure of the stature of the fullness of Christ." Eph 4:11-13

This book will be written in so many different languages of the world, that is what God instructed us

The Holy Spirit; the Third Person of the Godhead

to do, we will have it in Swahili, Russian, Chinese, Luganda, Spanish, Norwegian, French, Polish, Italian, Igbo, Ukrainian, Korean, Irish, Arabic, etc. The reason for this is to position us, the Children of God, to get all the help God has for us through the Holy Spirit.

God has sent me to you under this very powerful anointing, I am right in His presence with you now. The Lord God Almighty is illuminating our path at this very moment, because He loves us. This is your moment to shine out. The Holy Spirit, the Third Person of the Godhead, does desire to speak to you as well as lead you to deep things in God; you need to know that He speaks.

In the narrative in the book of Acts Chapter Thirteen, you notice that those prophets and teachers did not work against the leading of the Lord, but strived to obey the words of our Lord Jesus Christ concerning the Holy Spirit. "However, when He the Spirit of Truth is come. He will guide you into all truth......." John 16:13 No wonder the church of the book of Acts flowed in the power of God; people were healed, delivered, became 'Born Again' in big numbers. They shared what they

The Holy Spirit is Not an It: Has a Personality

had with one another, and none lacked among themselves. We need the leading of the Holy Spirit.

Those People Who Came to Convert Us, Became Converted Instead

Those four precious people who came to our door and eventually into our living room, ended up asking so many questions about the Person of the Holy Spirit. They became very interested in this scripture: "For it seemed good to the Holy Spirit, and to us to lay upon you no greater burden than these necessary things." Acts 15:28 Here you get a better glimpse of the nature of the Third Person of the Godhead concerning we, the Sheep, coming in agreement with Him. If you have to agree with anyone: you need to agree with the Holy Spirit, for He is the Spirit of Wisdom; Counsel of God; Knowledge; and the fear of the Lord. "There shall come forth a Rod from the stem of Jesse. And a Branch shall grow out of his roots. The Spirit of the LORD Shall rest upon Him. The Spirit of Wisdom and Understanding, The Spirit of Counsel and Might, The Spirit of Knowledge and of the Fear of the LORD." Is 11:1-2

The Holy Spirit; the Third Person of the Godhead

Precious one, those people who were holding the little Book of theirs, instead of the Holy Bible, when they walked in my house; who claimed to be part of a religious denomination, called the Church of Jesus Christ of the Latter Days and had a Mormon book: everything changed for better for them that day. They fell in love with the Holy Scriptures in the Holy Bible. They expressed a big desire to know more about the Word of God.

Their continence changed

You could see brightness on their faces, it was as if God had lifted His countenance over them. There was a Godly glean in their eyes, they said to me; 'This is amazing, what you are sharing with us; it is the truth!'

You might be in a situation that demands change, right now, possibly some group or persons gave you erroneous teachings about the Third Person of the God Head – The Holy Spirit. But, good news, that is why this book is in your hands, to get you back on course; to point you to the Word of God in the Holy Bible concerning the third Person of the Godhead, so that you may walk in agreement with God and be blessed. Those people who came to our house changed course, they gl-

The Holy is Not an It: Has a Personality

adly abandoned that erroneous little book of theirs and received Jesus Christ as their personal savior, later they joined a Bible-based Christ centered church, and today as I write this book, they are 'Born Again' Spirit filled believers.

The Holy Spirit points people to the Word of God in the Holy Bible. The Bible was written under the inspiration of the Third Person of the God Head and it takes the help of the Holy Spirit to interpret it. No little book should be handed over to the people of God in an effort to distract them from the Word of God. John testifies about this in the book of Revelation, Chapter Twenty, "For I testify to everyone who hears the words of this prophecy of this book; if anyone adds to these things, God will add to him the plagues that are written in this book, and if anyone takes away from the words of the book of this prophecy, God shall take away His part from the Book of Life, from the holy City, and from the things which are written in this book." Rev 21:18-19 Please love Jesus Christ and the Word of God, and let the Holy Spirit help you.

The Holy Spirit Gives Us What to Speak and Power Follows

One of the secrets of the manifestation of God's power

The Holy Spirit; the Third Person of the Godhead

in any worship service is one's willingness through the inner witness of the voice of the Holy Spirit to say as well as do what He gives us. Jesus Christ, the Son of the living God, laid it out very clearly that, when we are faced with a situation whereby we need to subdue opposition as well as deliver a word, spoken in a season: that the Third Person of the Godhead will not only give us what we need to speak but it will be God Himself speaking through us. "But when they deliver you up, do not worry about how or what you should speak. For it will be given to you in that hour what you should speak; "for it is not you who speaks, but the Spirit of your Father who speaks in you." Matt 10:19-2 0

Just reading that verse opens your eyes to the fundamental truth that the Third Person of the Godhead, the Holy Spirit, does speak as well as lead the children of God. No wonder we need to know the Holy Spirit. So that we live lives that pleases God, and end up reaping the benefits of His power revealed in our lives.

The Holy Spirit Helps Me and the Church through a Very Tough Situation in Kampala. Uganda – Africa.

The Holy Spirit is Not an It: Has a Personality

I was pastoring a church near Mawanda Road in Kamwokya, Kampala, in the Nation of Uganda, East Africa. The name of our church was Christian Faith Center, it was in the nineties, around 1994. There was a big move of God in the Body of Christ in Uganda. God's love through Jesus Christ was being preached in almost every town and city, so many were turning away from their own ways and ending up receiving Jesus Christ as their personal savior. We had an urge to give warning to the people concerning eternity. We had read the book of Ezekiel, Chapter Three, verses eighteen through nineteen. "Son of man I have made you a watchman for the house of Israel; therefore, hear a word from my mouth, and give them warning from me: "When I say to the wicked, you shall surely die," and you give them no warning nor Speak to warn the wicked from his wicked way to save his life, that same wicked man, shall die in his iniquity; but his blood I will require at your hand." Ezek 3:17-18 I personally took those words seriously, as if they were directly spoken to me by the Lord God Almighty.

At our church, we had services every day in the evening, as well as services on Saturday morning and Sunday morning. The power of God was gloriously in

The Holy Spirit; the Third Person of the Godhead

Manifestation in those worship services, people came from everywhere to hear the Word of God taught under the anointing of the Holy Spirit. We even had a night service where we ministered to God every Friday from 11:00pm to 1:00am. Those who wanted to stay and pray further, would stay in the Sanctuary waiting on God through prayer until the dawning of the day. Our church building was not very sophisticated, it was a big house, that had several rooms and a big living room area, which we ended up using for church services. There was also an extended structure attached to the building where people sat while attending services. People would fill up the entire space. I would gladly say that this property was the most visited piece of real estate in that part of the town.

Someone Reports Us to the Police for Praising and Worshiping God!

Some people near our place of worship did not like all the activity that was going on at our church. People would also come from all over the country for counseling every day from morning to evening. Church

The Holy Spirit is Not an It: Has a Personality

people would tell everyone, 'Go to that church over there in Kamwokya and God will bless you, those people will pray for you in the Name of Jesus Christ and you will receive a miracle.' So people would come from Masaka, Mukono, Jinja, Entebbe, Ggaba, Soroti, Gulu, Lira, Mbarara, Kyotera, etc., to be prayed for. I had a very anointed team of ministers with me: Pastor Abbey Mukwana, pastor Baguma, Prophet Charles Galabuzi, Pastor/Teacher Matthew, Pastor Sarah, Nawagaba, Evangelist Edegar, Apostle Ddamba, Pastor Sam, Pastor Grace, Pastor Kazibwe, Minister Mary, Evangelist Edith, etc., the list goes on and on. When we prayed for the people of God, miracles occurred so that there was a lot of jubilation at our church.

Some of the neighboring residents did not like what was going on so they brought a lawsuit against me and the church, they wanted to shut the church down. They claimed that unknown people are coming in their area and they could be bandits or just bad people; the real problem was with these people; they did not want a change from their wicked ways. It was all about them. It was all 'me, me, me and I alone, if I can't manipulate

The Holy Spirit; the Third Person of the Godhead

the people of God, then I should silence them!'

Well, as the pastor of the church, I had to deal with that challenge, so the day came for me and the church elders to go to the District Police Post to appear before the District Police Commander and the Detectives, to respond to the malicious accusations of our opponents. They were there at the time we arrived, anxiously waiting for us.

We arrive at the police post

I went with about thirty people from our church. It was a big police post on Kira Road in Kamwokya. They also had jail cells where they kept prisoners. The Police Post was located in Ntinda, Kampala, it was a town next to Kamwokya. Our opponents were already seated, and they had pleaded with the District Police Commander to have us arrested, but he had told them that he could not do that without evidence of criminal activity. He had to hear from both sides.

The accusations were read to us; that these people are conducting an illegal gathering every day; whereby unknown people come from everywhere to pray and

The Holy Spirit is Not an It: Has a Personality

Praise God as well as dance for the Lord. Some of them come and knock on our doors, asking us to become 'Born Again,' even though we already have our religions.

The District Police Commander said to me, 'Please can you stop those prayers immediately and shut down that church.' There is something that I want to bring to your attention here: our church was legally authorized to conduct church services all over Uganda by the Ugandan Government, which our assailants did not want to know.

The Holy Spirit Gives Me What to Say

I answered back and said; 'I can't shut down that church, I am just the Pastor of the congregation; I am an under shepherd; Jesus Christ is the Founder of the church, and the Shepherd,' that was a shock to my opponents, even the District Police Commander was shaken up. He said to me; 'Just tell the people not to come to worship or to be prayed for.' I said to him, 'I can't do that, I can't fight against God, my job is to serve the people of God faithfully, not to chase them

The Holy Spirit; the Third Person of the Godhead

away from God's Sanctuary.' He nodded his head, went outside, and consulted with some of his advisers, came back in the room and said, 'I was planning to arrest you, but I don't know where to begin; you go and your people, I will continue to look further into this matter!' Well, that was the last time I ever heard from that man concerning that issue. The church continued to grow and many were added daily to the Body of Christ. We did a lot of person to person evangelism in that region, we had around ten thousand people born again. Thank God for the Third Person of the Godhead, the Holy Spirit, who gave me the words to say that Day.

The Holy Spirit Reveals the Things of God to Us

In this book, we are obtaining knowledge about the Spirit of God, so that we may be able to yield to the leading of God; for He is God Himself. We are gaining an appreciation of His person, as well as celebrating Him as one who is part of our lives. We recognize the fact that the Holy Spirit is not an it, but one who does feel what we experience and understands our trials and temptations in this life. He hears our concerns; He does

The Holy Spirit is Not an It: Has a Personality

The Son. Many perpetrators of those erroneous teachings carry big titles and big degrees as well as diplomas from their own schools; not the lifelong school of the Holy Spirit, whereby the key to learning and receiving sound doctrine is yielding to the leading of the Holy Spirit, who alone knows the things of God. I ran into one of those preachers, he told me that they don't read any other book whereby the writer acknowledges God as a trinity, that is God the Father, God the Son and God the Holy Spirit. He explained to me further that the name of God is Jesus Christ. Well, it sounds very interesting when you look at it from an intellectual perspective but when you look at the scriptures, Jesus Christ Himself said that there is God the Father, that's why He asked us in The Lord's Prayer, to pray 'Our Father who art in Heaven, hallowed be thy name...' you will find this prayer in Matthew chapter six starting from verse nine to verse thirteen. In this prayer, you pray to God the Father in the Name of Jesus Christ, so there has to be a clear distinction between the two. Jesus also says in the book of John, Chapter Sixteen, verse thirteen, "However, when He, the Spirit of truth, has come, He will guide you into all truth; for He will not speak on His own authority, but whatever

The Holy Spirit; the Third Person of the Godhead

He hears He will speak; and He will tell you things to come." John 16:13 This scripture clearly identifies the Third Person of the Godhead as someone with His own personality within the Godhead. So, beloved of God, if you have been caught into this strife and conflict in regard to the Name of Jesus Christ, please flee, as quickly as you can from those groups, for you can't move forward in God, while you are spending all of your energy on things that are divisive. The ways of God are pure and clean, His yoke is easy and His burden is light. "Come to Me, all you who labor and are heavy laden, and I will give you rest. "Take my yoke upon you and learn from Me, for I am gentle and lowly in heart, and you will find rest for your souls. "For My yoke is easy and my burden is light." Matt 11:28-30 The truth of God's word sets one free and that is why this book has been written, to help you know the truth.

Simon Offers Money to the Apostles to Buy the Holy Spirit!

Simon had astonished the people of Samaria with his sorceries for a long time; they even referred to him as the great power of God! In the book of Acts, Chapter

The Holy Spirit is Not an It: Has a Personality

Eight, Verse Eleven. People thought that this man was that great; they were fascinated by this man's acts. Even today, many people are fascinated by personalities of people as well as their human deeds. Sometimes we get carried away by what is not real and not even from God. Things without substance.

The substance is, Jesus came in flesh, was born of a virgin woman, Mary, into this world, taught the way of God to us, suffered in our stead on the rugged cross, died for our sins, and God raised Him up from the dead on the third day by the Holy Spirit. "But if the Spirit of Him who raised Jesus from the dead dwells in you, He who raised Christ from the dead will also give life to your mortal bodies through His Spirit who dwells in you." Rom 8:11

Here is something astonishing about the man Simon the sorcery, a wicked celebrity during that time. He saw miracles, wonders and signs happening as Philip preached the Gospel of our Lord Jesus Christ. "Then Philip went down to the City of Samaria and preached Christ to them." Acts 8:5

Let me teach a little bit here, we will continue on Simon after this: -

The secret to the glory of God as well as the power of

The Holy Spirit the Third Person of the Godhead

God in our lives is to live lives that glorify God. Always remembering that the Third Person of the Godhead, the Holy Spirit is the one that manifests the things of God; now one of the keys to operating in the miraculous is to line up with the likes of God. This is very well spelled out in the Gospel of St. John Chapter Sixteen, verse fourteen, Jesus said this, "He will glorify Me, for He will take what is mine and declare it to you. "All things that the Father has are Mine. Therefore, I said that He will take of Mine and declare it to you." John 16:14-15

When your desire is to see Jesus Christ the Son of the Living God glorified in your life through living in accordance with the Word of God, and for a preacher if your desire is to preach a Jesus centered message, that which is from the Holy Bible and lifts up Jesus Christ for the world to see, that brings you in agreement with the Holy Spirit: God gets pleased and what follows are miracles, wonders and signs as well as peace that surpasses understanding, divine protection, joy unspeakable, anointing, holy laughter, greater love, etc.

The reason why miracles, wonders and signs took place in Samaria when Phillip preached; who was one

The Holy Spirit is Not an It: Has a Personality

of the seven who were chosen and set apart to serve the people of God, because they were full of wisdom, faith and the Holy Spirit was, due to his being led by the Spirit of God to preach Jesus. As much as he was a blessing to the people of Samaria, he was already a blessing to the children of God. In the book of Acts, Chapter 6 verse Five, the word of the Lord says, "And the saying pleased the whole multitude. And they chose Stephen, a man full of faith and the Holy Spirit, and Philip, Prochorus, Nicanor, Timon, Parmenas, and Nicolas, a proselyte from Antioch." Acts 6:5

Philip was yielded to the leading of the Holy Spirit and desired to see Jesus Christ glorified, the previous verse reveals this "Now therefore, seek out from among you seven men of good reputation, full of the Holy Spirit and wisdom whom we may appoint over this business." Acts 6:31

Unusual miracles, wonders and signs through my life and our church services

I have operated in the miraculous, so many people have been healed through the anointing of God on my

The Holy Spirit: The Third Person of the Godhead

Life and ministry; they have been healed from cancer, diabetes, Aids, arthritis, pneumonia, blindness, blood diseases, tumors disappearing, hearing restored, etc. I have witnessed God do miracles through the course of my call to preach the gospel, and I would like to let you know that all that happened by the Holy Spirit of God. The key has been, I strive to do all that I know to glorify Jesus Christ, and that unlocks the supernatural in our services. God is no respecter of persons. When we move ourselves out of the way, and let God have His way, we will always see His glory in our lives as well as our churches. To put it in a very simple way: Let 'I' decrease and God increase.

There are times when we would be worshiping the Lord God Almighty in the Name of Jesus Christ our Lord, that the Glory of God would manifest among us so tangibly and it was such a blessed moment, that everyone would gladly say, 'surely, the presence of the Lord is in this place'. People ended up getting jobs, houses, vehicles, scholarships to colleges, promotions at work, receiving creative miracles, deliverance from demons and demonic activity, and most important, a lot

The Holy Spirit is not an It: Has a Personality

received Jesus Christ as their personal Savior, and others ended up filled with the Holy Spirit with evidence of speaking in tongues. None of this would have happened, if we were not yielded to the leading of the Third Person of the Godhead – The Holy Spirit.

I will be continuing to share about what happened in the City of Samaria concerning their perception of God. As they tried their best to interpret the works of Simon the Sorcerer, but I am going to go ahead and bring you into one of our services where an amazing miracle took place, through the Gift of Word of Knowledge by the Holy Spirit.

The Holy Spirit speaks to me to Call out a Miracle by Word of Knowledge

I was at the pulpit teaching the Word of God under a very beautiful anointing, there were about four hundred people in the sanctuary. People were glued to the words I spoke as I gave references to the scriptures that supported what the Lord God gave me to minister that day. Then suddenly, I felt a tangible presence of

The Holy Spirit; the Third Person of the Godhead

God on my left hand, it was as if someone was touching me, it was a power touch; electrical. When that happened, I knew something very good was going to be done by God to His people. Then the Holy Spirit of God, spoke to me to say this, 'Someone is being healed of diabetes right now.' The moment these words came out of my mouth, the power of God fell on a man that was about ten meters from where I was standing; he shook under that power, swayed due to that power, you could see the effect of that divine presence all over him. His body jerked and he fell over. This dear man was vibrating under the power of God. It was as if a live electrical circuit was going through his body. The ushers rushed to his side, where this precious blessed man was lying and watched closely as he received his healing.

Healing in Manifestation

Now, after about five minutes, the man rose to his feet and started praising God loudly. He was a big and tall man in his early sixties. This man started shouting, 'I am healed, all the pain is gone, I am healed from diabetes; the power of God has gone through my entire

The Holy Spirit is Not an It: Has a Personality

body, and I know I have been healed. The whole place went into praise, the more He praised God the more the Glory of God increased in that place. People ended up receiving healings from various ailments without any of us ministers who were present that day, laying our hands on them. Miracles broke out in our midst. What is astounding, the more that man glorified God for his miracle healing in the Name of Jesus Christ, the more the power of God increased.

This man thanked Jesus Christ for His grace to him, and in the process everyone benefited. I could feel the Holy Presence of God increasing on me every time he was thankful. It reminded me of Revelation Chapter Five, Verse Thirteen to Fourteen: "And every creature which is in heaven and on the earth and under the earth and such as are in the sea and all that are in them. I heard saying: "Blessing and honor and glory and power. Be to Him who sits on the throne! And to the lamb, forever and ever!" Rev 5:13-14

This man was completely healed. He did go and was checked by his doctors and they came to a conclusion that a miracle had happened in that man's life that caused him to be free from Diabetes. All this took place because I let the Holy Spirit have His way in that service.

Back to Simon who had practiced sorcery, previously

What is interesting about the narrative of Simon in the Eighth Chapter of Acts, verse Thirteen is this: "Then Simon himself also believed and when he was baptized he continued with Philip, and was amazed, seeing the miracles and signs which were done." Acts 8:13

This man saw the signs, the miracles and the wonders, but the problem was, he never understood the Person of the Holy Spirit, he did not really know who God was. He was fascinated by the works of God, but he needed to know the God of those works. You will get a glimpse of my point when you continue reading down the road.

The Bible says, when the Apostles came down from Jerusalem to Samaria after hearing that the people in

The Holy Spirit is Not an It: Has a Personality

Samaria had received the gospel, and laid hands on them to receive the Holy Spirit; Simon saw the wonder of the people receiving the Holy Spirit. When he saw that, he offered the apostles money to give him that power, so that when he lays hands on any one, they may receive the Holy Spirit. "And when Simon saw through the laying on of the apostle's hands, the Holy Spirit was given. He offered them money saying, "Give me this power also, that anyone on whom I lay hands may receive the Holy Spirit." Acts 8:18-19

Just reading those scriptures lets you know the problem of not having the knowledge of God. "My people are destroyed for lack of knowledge. Because you have rejected knowledge I also will reject you from being priest for me; Because you have forgotten the law of your God, I also will forget your children." Hos 4:6 Many these days are trying to treat God the Holy Spirit like He is an it, they do all the talking, the commanding, the acting: it is like a show without Heavenly power. It is as if it is all about themselves, which is not true, and should not be so. We have to know God; God loves us; Jesus died for us on the Cross; the Holy Spirit of God is in our lives to guide us. We are God's children.

The Holy Spirit; the Third Person of the Godhead

We can't afford powerlessness any more. We are living in perilous times. We need to let God have all of us. "But Peter said to him, "Your money perish with you, because you thought that the gift of God could be purchased with money! "You have neither part nor portion in this matter, for your heart is not right in the Sight of God. Repent therefore of this your wickedness and pray God, if perhaps the thought of your heart may be forgiven you." Acts 8:20-22

Precious one, this language used by Peter is very strong; there is an element in it that pointed to Simon, blaspheming the Holy Spirit, and the only remedy to his act was repentance. If you are doing things that are not right before God, just repent; that is the only way to get back to course, go ahead and find a church where people are Spirit filled and do honor God. "Therefore putting away lying, 'let each one of you speak truth with his neighbor, "For we are members of one another. "Be angry and do not sin." Do not let the sun go down on your wrath, nor give place to the devil. Let him who stole, steal no longer, but rather let him labor, working with his hands what is good, that he may have some-

The Holy Spirit is Not an It: Has a Personality

thing to give him who has need. Let no corrupt word proceed out of your mouth but what is good for necessary edification, that it may give grace to the hearers. And do not grieve the Holy Spirit of God, by whom you were sealed for the day of redemption." Eph 4:25-30

This book is in your hands today because God love you. God may not like wicked acts, but loves all of us. This is your moment to shine; this is your appointed time to rise higher, that is to lay hold of the leading of the Spirit of God. It is time to acknowledge that you are not self-made, but someone by the name of Jesus Christ did become the atonement for our sins, and that the Third Person of the Godhead; is real help through this Christian life journey on earth and we need all His help.

Pillar Scriptures -:
There are a number of scriptures in the Bible that mostly have to do with living and walking a life that is pleasing to God. Those scriptures contain holy counsel, that is being given to us, the Body of Christ, by the Holy Spirit of God through various and anointed vessels.

The Holy Spirit; the Third Person of the Godhead

These scriptures have a lot to do with being in agreement with the Holy Spirit; honoring God in our day to day conduct and living by the word of God.

The Word of God says in the Epistle of First Peter Chapter Three from verse ten to verse twelve, "For "He who would love life, And see good days, let him refrain his tongue from evil, And his lips from speaking deceit. Let him turn away from evil and do good: Let him seek peace and pursue it. For the eyes of the LORD are on the righteous. And His ears are open to their prayers; But the face of the Lord is against those who do evil." I Peter 3:10-13

When you say yes Lord to that counsel in the Word of God; you are then lining up with that which pleases the Holy Spirit. Those words were written down under the inspiration of God the Holy Spirit, they bring the will of God to us. Light is shone in our path, So that we are not resisted by God but guided as dear children. "Likewise you younger people, submit yourselves to your elders. Yes, all of you be submissive to one another, and be clothed with humility, for 'God resists the proud, But gives grace to the humble.' Therefore, humble yourselves under the mighty hand of God that

The Holy Spirit is Not an It; Has a Personality

He may exalt you in due time." I Peter 5:5-6. Beloved, that is Godly counsel. When we adhere to those sayings from the Word of God; we do please God Almighty, and He does manifest His Glory on our lives. We believers are supposed to be a people of praise and power. We can pray and then decree things on earth and they come to pass, for the Lord God can put words in our mouths; words that are creative and heavenly. "And they were all filled with the Holy Spirit and began to speak with other tongues as the Spirit gave them utterance." Acts 2:4

The counsel in those scriptures points us to a life style that is void of behaviors, that cause the teacher; the third person of the Godhead; to be grieved. That is why you need to be part of a Christian assembly whereby the Word of God is being taught accurately so that you may know how to conduct yourself before the Lord God Almighty, for He is a Holy God. No wonder the Word of God says, 'Be Holy for I am Holy'.

The Holy Spirit, Versus the Description; the Holy Ghost!!!

Many of us growing up were rendered to have some

The Holy Spirit; the Third Person of the Godhead

concerns about the word, 'ghost.' Any time that word was mentioned, our hair stood up on our backs! - In case we have some out there! Even in the Gospels when our Lord Jesus Christ came to His disciples walking on water, which for some reason they were not expecting, the first impression they expressed was fear that it might be a ghost. They become so troubled that they cried out and said, 'It is a ghost!' Jesus Himself had to admonish them that it was Him and not a ghost.

The Lord God Almighty has led me to address this issue worldwide in these scripts so that all of us may be on the same page concerning the Holy Spirit.

So many things had been written about ghosts and many of the experiences people claimed to have had with these 'spirits' manifesting in bodily form were horrible. ghosts were mostly depicted as evil, controlling spiritual beings that imposed their wicked acts on people. ghosts were associated with witchcraft, as of today as I speak to you in this very eye opening book. In the Western World, many people celebrate something called, 'Halloween.' On that day, and during that week, costumes and portraits as well as figures that look horrible and scary are displayed in neighborhoods,

The Holy Spirit is Not an It: Has a Personality

on houses and cars with inscriptions 'ghosts'! Some connect that word with dead people coming out of the tomb in the cemetery to scare those who are alive, and because of all of that confusion, when some people hear the word, 'Holy Ghost' they shy away from that for suddenly they are afraid.

The disciples nearly rejected a Jesus walking on the water, presuming that it might be a ghost. Thanks to God, they later received Him very gladly. Even Peter had to say that if it is you Lord, command me to come to you walking on water and He said, 'come.'

Please, don't turn away from the Holy Spirit, He is God; He is the Spirit of God, the Holy Ghost is full of love, is for us – not against us.

This has to be very well understood. That is why you have this book in your hands, for God loves you.

A Pastor tries to burn Bibles with the word 'Holy Ghost.'

There was a pastor in a certain country who for some reason became carried away concerning the word, 'Holy Ghost.' This man, present in the 21st Century had

The Holy Spirit; the Third Person of the Godhead

a church with a good number of followers. Some were along his priestly obligations to the believers, he came to a conclusion that the word 'Holy Ghost' should not have been in the Bibles. This pastor started asking Christians anywhere to send him Bibles that had the Old English word, 'Holy Ghost' as the description of the Holy Spirit, that he should burn them.

It was a very controversial situation. Some thought he was right, others went to court and opened law suits against him, for being very unreasonable to that extent. Many who knew who the Holy Spirit is, referred to as the Holy Ghost in many of the Old English Bibles, became saddened at the extent of the confusion that it was creating.

Beloved, I am one of those preachers who love referring the Third Person of the Godhead as the 'Holy Spirit' with clear understanding that the Old English Bible never meant harm to use the phrase, 'Holy Ghost' when they described the Helper. They even put the word 'Holy' in the description of Him to make a clear distinction between this Third Person of the Godhead and anything else that people would throw in there to cause chaos. As I write this book, most of the English

The Holy Spirit is Not an It: Has a Personality

Bibles no longer use the phrase 'Holy Ghost' anymore, for there has been a deliberate attempt to make the English Language lighter and easier to work with. You also need to know that God has not given us a spirit of fear, but of power, love and a sound mind. "For God has not given us a spirit of fear, but of power and of love and of a sound mind." 2 Tim. 1:7

To some Saints, the phrase, 'Holy Ghost' in the Old English Bible does not bother them, but as a pastor I prefer to make it easier on the new converts and to those who have been born again for a while, by calling the Third Person of the Godhead: The Holy Spirit. Even preaching to the yet to be converted, it would be a good idea to somehow use the word 'Holy Spirit' instead of 'Holy Ghost.' However, I leave this to the preacher because there is nothing wrong with the word, 'Holy Ghost,' when substance is upheld.

Burning Bibles because the 'Holy Spirit' is referred to as the 'Holy Ghost' it is not necessary!!!!!!!!

The Holy Spirit is called, 'Omwoyo Omutukuvu' in Luganda, a language that is spoken by so many in

The Holy Spirit; the Third Person of the Godhead

Uganda, East Africa. The people in Russia may have a different word for the Holy Spirit, but you getting up and require peoples Holy Bibles to be burnt, because the naming or description of God in a different language is not familiar to you, is not necessary; just a distraction.

The Holy Spirit referred to as the Holy Ghost in some Old English Bibles, is the same Third Person of the Godhead and is loving and gentle.

The disciples terrified, thinking Jesus was a ghost-let us look at this incidence a little bit more!

A very interesting incidence occurred in the Holy Bible around Chapter Fourteen of the Gospel of Matthew from verse twenty-two to verse twenty-eight. When Jesus Christ, the Second Person of the Godhead came towards His disciples walking on the water. These people had traveled with the Lord Jesus Christ to many places, and had been partakers of His numerous miracles. In this incidence, there deep fear for the unfamiliar was unmasked, especially in a situation like this where their fear of ghosts was portrayed like some people today. They were in the boat in the middle of

The Holy Spirit is Not an It: Has a Personality

the sea and the winds were contrary to their course. These disciples could see danger all around them, and somehow they could associate this bad experience to 'ghosts,' for when Jesus approached them, walking on water, they cried out thinking it was a 'ghost.' "Immediately Jesus made His disciples get into the boat and go before Him to the other side, while He sent the multitude away, And when He had sent the multitude away, He went up on the mountain by Himself to pray. Now when evening came, He was alone there. But the boat was now in the middle of the sea tossed by the waters for the wind was contrary. Now in the fourth watch of the night, Jesus went to them walking on the sea. And when the disciples saw Him walking on the sea, they were troubled, saying, 'It is a ghost!' And they cried out for fear, but immediately Jesus spoke to them saying, "Be of good cheer! It is I: do not be afraid." Matt 14:22-27

Child of God, the Holy Spirit is for you and by you, upon you, for your good and safety. He is not trying to slay you! He is interested in blessing you and bringing you to a Godly plateau. Do not be at all afraid of the Holy Spirit. He is a loving comforter. He is not a ghost.

The Holy Spirit; the Third Person of the Godhead

Perception matters: wrong perception of anything can lead to rejection of that particular thing. When the disciples in the boat at the sea perceived wrongly, who was coming towards them, walking on the sea, they withdrew into themselves in fear. Jesus had to assure them that it was Him; their beloved Savior and Lord, the one who was with them earlier before they entered the boat. Peter wanted to make sure it was the Second Person of the Godhead, not a ghost, "And Peter answered Him and said; "Lord, if it is You command me to come to You on the water." So he said, "Come." And when Peter had come down out of the boat, he walked on the water to go to Jesus." Matt 14:28-30

Know who the Holy Spirit is

Like Peter, you can submit to the leading of the Holy Spirit of God and tap into exploits. Peter having confirmed that it was Jesus Christ talking to him, he quickly sought to operate at a higher level; he stepped out of the boat and walked on the water. It is time for you to step out of the boat of unbelief and go ahead and receive the Baptism of the Holy Spirit with evidence of speaking in tongues; it is time for you to have a good

The Holy Spirit is Not an It: Has a Personality

Fellowship with the Third Person of the Godhead. I would not have written all the books I have been graced by God to write if I had rejected the communion of the Holy Spirit. You are for miracles, wonders and signs, "Here am I and the children whom the LORD has given me! We are for signs and wonders in Israel. From the LORD of hosts, who dwells in Mount Zion." Is 8:18

Slain in the Spirit Verses Blessed in the Spirit

When the power of the Holy Spirit comes upon you, believer, you get blessed not slain. Wrong application of slogans causes confusion in regard to good cause, words matter. The presence of God on your life is a blessing; when you are prayed for and the power of God goes through your body mightily, it does you good and it is for your good. For the Spirit of God does give life to your mortal body. "But if the Spirit of Him who raised Jesus from the dead dwells in you, He who raised Christ from the dead will also give life to your mortal bodies through His Spirit who dwells in you." Rom 8:11

I have had a lot of success praying with people to receive the Baptism of the Holy Spirit with evidence of speaking in tongues, through saying words that are in line with the nature of the Holy Spirit; for the Holy

The Holy Spirit; the Third Person of the Godhead

Spirit is a comforter; is compassionate; is a helper; is a teacher, "But the Helper, the Holy Spirit, whom the Father will send in My name, He will teach you all things, and bring to your remembrance all things that I said to you." John 14:26

The power of God slays demons and diseases, breaks yokes, and removes burdens.

The Holy Spirit Guides

He leads you into all truth. God is not forcing truth on you, He wants to help you see it as well as receive it. It is God who gave you a free will and He desires you exercising that will right. Demons try to forcibly gain evil control over God's people, they transgress.

But God the Holy Spirit desires to guide you into all truth; He tenderly leads you to green pastures in God. "For as many as are led by the Spirit of God, these are sons of God. For you did not receive the spirit of bondage again to fear, but you received the Spirit of adoption by whom we cry out, "Abba. Father." The Spirit Himself bears witness with our spirit that we are children of God." Rom 8:14-16

The Holy Spirit is Not an It: Has a Personality

The number one way how the Third Person of the Godhead leads us, is through inner witness, it is normally a gentle inner conviction or knowing of the will of God for us concerning anything. This shines out very well when we endeavor to know God's word. You tend to have a strong inner conviction or knowing of what is right for any situation, and many times, it is in line with the Word of God – The Holy Bible.

We should not be afraid of the Holy Spirit. He is God himself: and is looking out for the best for us. He speaks after Jesus Christ, who speaks after God the Father; these three are one, but functioning differently in the redemption plan of man. We need all of them together and their unique roles in our lives.

Communion of the Holy Spirit

Look at this very interesting scripture with me in regard to the three persons of the Godhead and their unique roles. "The grace of our Lord Jesus Christ, and the love of God, and the communion of the Holy Spirit be with you all, Amen." 2 Cor 13:14 Beloved, in here, when it came to the Holy Spirit, the word used here is

The Holy Spirit; the Third Person of the Godhead

Fellowship/Communion: One you communicate with daily; one you communicate with in line with Godly counsel and mercies; a friend; a person you give your ear to and affections. No wonder the Apostles at Jerusalem when they wrote to the brethren in the book of Acts Chapter Five regarding the issues of circumcision, whereby some men were confusing grace with law; trying to have the brethren circumcised as one of the requirements or the necessity for them to be born again. The Apostles rejected that erroneous teaching and in their letter to the brethren they included this very powerful statement: "For it seemed good to the Holy Spirit, and to us, to lay upon you no greater burden than these necessary things; that you abstain from things offered to idols, from blood, from things strangled, and from sexual immorality. If you keep yourselves from this, you will do well. Farewell." Acts 15:28-29

Through the Holy Spirit, your burdens are lightened. Yokes are loosed from you, and He does it with such precision that no human being can attain. He is the guide you need in life, and the one who understands you very well. He is the teacher. Always present with us. Anybody trying to teach the Word of God without yielding to the leading of the Holy Spirit ends up

The Holy Spirit is Not an It: Has a Personality

confused and confusing others. I have run into those who claim that Jehovah is God, and that there is no God the Son, nor God the Holy Spirit, but in the same breath, they claim that Jesus Christ is the Son of God; they go further to insist that the Holy Spirit is just some power, God used to create. These same teachers, when you ask them whether a child of a human being, should rightly be called a human being as well, they say of course. Then why should God's only begotten son not be called God as well? They just look at you and seem confused at hearing that.

The Word of God was written under the inspiration of the Holy Spirit, trying to interpret it, as well as explain it without a life fully submitted to Jesus Christ and whereby your only desire is to see Jesus Christ glorified is futile. For what happens, you become a teacher who draws from your natural means and worse could be influenced by the Devil to say things which contradicts the Word of God. Endeavoring to preach a supernatural Gospel that requires the enlightenment of the Holy Spirit, void of submission to Him, turns into legalism, no wonder Jesus Christ told His disciples not to leave Jerusalem without having received the promise of the Father – God the Holy Spirit, the Third Person of the Godhead.

3

IT IS
THE HOLY SPIRIT
WHO
BAPTIZES US INTO THE
BODY OF CHRIST

"For by one Spirit we were all baptized into one body. Whether Jews or Greeks; whether slaves or free and have all been made to drink into one Spirit." I Cor 12:13

Beloved, this book is not a fiction novel. This script has been written to bring action on your part. A believer is supposed to be a commissioner on earth for the Kingdom of God. We are God's ambassadors. "Now then we are ambassadors for Christ, as though God were pleading through us: we implore you in Christ's behalf, be reconciled to God." 2 Cor 5:20 We are supposed to have a good understanding of what is at stake, concern-

-155-

The Holy Spirit; the Third Person of the Godhead

ing the salvation of the souls of men through the witness of the Holy Spirit of God. You have to be able to help someone who is off track, on the way to Hell; to desist from their wicked activities and turn their lives over to Jesus Christ, so that Heaven may become their eternal home.

You and I are right in the presence of God Almighty, receiving enlightenment for the course of action needed to be taken in our lives as citizens of heaven residing on earth. "For our citizenship is in heaven, from which we also eagerly wait for the Savior, the Lord Jesus Christ." Phil 3:20 God's anointing is coming on us strong right now and we are receiving revelation knowledge about the Third Person of the Godhead – The Holy Spirit, so that we can be effective, anointed, divinely empowered, full of faith and good works.

Beloved, at the moment one dies, everything else may not matter, except the answer to this question: 'Did you receive the free gift to humanity for salvation of the soul from God – the Lord Jesus Christ?' I have performed a lot of funerals, and have been able to be briefed of the achievements of those deceased while on earth; what they used to own, which schools they atten-

The Holy Spirit, Baptizes Us into the Body of Christ

ded, their political status as well as their academic achievements. I do listen to all that very humbly, as a pastor and a servant of the Lord God Almighty, but deep in my heart, I carefully await to hear whether the person was born again. "Jesus answered and said to him, "Most assuredly I say to you, unless one is born again he cannot see the Kingdom of God." John 3:3

Hell is Real: You don't want to Go There

As you are reading this book, you may be part of a group of people who laugh about the fact that Hell is real. Someone may have taught you who lacks understanding in the things of God, that God is so loving that He can't send anybody to Hell, you just continue on your Christ-less path, and everything will be fine! Please, in case you have been captivated through those kinds of teachings, it is time to free those teachings and embrace Jesus Christ as your personal savior; Hell is real. You don't want to spend your eternal life there. The day your spirit comes out of your body due to death, you will either be present in Hell or in Heaven.

Jesus Taught a Lot About Hell

The Holy Spirit; the Third Person of the Godhead

Jesus Chris, the third person of the Godhead taught so much about Hell. Just reading His words lets you know that God Almighty does not want anybody to go to that place. "If your right eye causes you to sin, pluck it out and cast it from you; for it is more profitable for you that one of your members perish, then for your whole body to be cast into Hell." Matt 5:29

I was one time talking to a preacher in a big city in the U.S.A., it was around 2006. He was part of a big church with a property that seats approximately 5,000 people and that church had been around for quite some time. I visited the pastor of that place with a friend, a pastor from West Virginia, in the U.S.A. This man of God was a God lover and a God seeker.

The Preacher Tells Us that there Is No Hell!

As we sat down in that very, very beautiful building in the pastor's office, this preacher who was the senior pastor of that church, started talking to us about the goodness of God, and went to the extent of telling us that there is no Hell. He said that God loves everybody so much that there can't be a Hell. This person continued to communicate to us the erroneous teaching

-158-

The Holy Spirit Baptizes Us into the Body of Christ

that the idea of Hell is man invented, to scare people and keep them under human control. You may be wondering why all this is analyzed in this book, especially if you are already born again. The answer is, you are being equipped for the work of ministry. "And He Himself gave some to be apostles, some prophets, some evangelists, and some pastors and teachers for the equipping of the Saints for the work of ministry, for the edification of the Body of Christ till we all come to the unity of faith and of the knowledge of the Son of God, to a perfect man, to the measure of Christ, that we should no longer be children, tossed to and from and carried about with every wind of doctrine, by the trickery of man in the cunning craftiness of deceitful plotting." Eph 4:11-14 You have to know the word of God in order to resist the devil as well as help others not to go to Hell – Hell is bad.

This Person had a PHD in Bible Theology from their religious group university

This preacher seemed very interested in letting us know that there is no Hell. This pastor talked to us with a big smile on his face; went further and informed us that in their church they had 7,000 adult members, whom they teach positive thinking as well as spiritual

The Holy Spirit; the Third Person of the Godhead

meditation from the scriptures. I really think that right here you are graciously acknowledging the fact that we need the help of the Holy Spirit. This person also said that in their doctrine, they tell people that man is not a sinner originally, that the concept of sin is not positive to humanity; but is invented by people to make others feel less!!!

Well, I asked this 'Doctor' about the story in Genesis concerning the fall of man, he said that, that is a figurative story, it is not reality. My pastor friend and I were perplexed. We looked at this misled man, with our mouth wide open, we gazed at him in disbelief. This teacher went further to tell us that Jesus Christ is Lord but there are many ways to come to God. That is why, in their church, they believe in universalism. I asked him, 'When people die, what happens?' This person said their spirits just hang around here, for this is heaven, and nobody goes to Hell, for no one has sinned.

This group had many other places of worship around the world and they all taught similar doctrine of universalism. Lastly, I asked this individual, 'Who is the Holy Spirit?' The answer this pastor gave us is this; that the Holy Spirit is a force from God, like electricity or heat, maybe light: it is not God. When this preacher

The Holy Spirit, Baptizes us into the Body of Christ

said that, I then saw the reason why this individual was in such very bad shape doctrine wise, and needed urgent help to get off that disastrous course, for surely I could see Hell wide open to receive this person. If you know people who have been taught that way, try to talk to them about the free gift of salvation; those people need to receive Jesus Christ as their personal savior. The Holy Spirit is with you, He will give you the words to say, for if anyone says that Jesus is Lord, but does not believes what He says in the Holy Bible, nor believe that Heaven and Hell are real places whereby God desires that none should perish, that person needs to get born again – that is to receive Jesus Christ as their personal Lord and Savior.

Anyone who denies that Jesus Christ came in flesh and taught us about the Kingdom of God; suffered and died on the cross for our sins, then rose from the dead after three days for our justification, that person regardless of how many titles are before their name, is not worthy paying heed to. That person needs to be instructed in the ways of God and needs the help of the Holy Spirit urgently. The Bible says that we have to trust the Lord our God with all of our hearts and not lean on just our understanding. Find this in Proverbs 3:5.

The Holy Spirit; the Third Person of the Godhead

"Trust in the Lord with all your heart, And lean not on your own understanding; In all your ways acknowledge Him, And He shall direct your paths." Prov 3:5-6 When we acknowledge God in our lives and accept His word ion the Holy Bible, then we place ourselves in a position of obtaining supernatural help to carry out His will. We cease to be self-contradicting for the Helper; the Holy Spirit enables us divinely to see the way, and that way is Jesus Christ – the Word of the Living God.

Back to Baptism

The word Baptismal means to immerse; to dip into; to cause to be submerged by something, either water or something else. This word Baptism, appears in the Bible concerning very crucial subjects dealing with the state of the human race, and for that reason, let us look at this incidences, briefly.

The Three Baptisms: -

The first baptism – towards becoming a believer.

This Baptism is so crucial for anyone to be part of the Kingdom of God. Jesus one time in the Gospel, was preaching to a large crowd of people in the Book of

The Holy Spirit, Baptizes Us into the Body of Christ

John, Chapter 6 from verse forty-eight to verse sixty-seven, the Lord spoke to this crowd that was so energized after they partook of the miracle whereby Jesus took five barley loaves of bread and two small fish and ended up feeding thousands miraculously. These same people followed Christ keenly, jubilant that they had found the messiah they needed, which so far was alright. After a while, when they found Him again, He started teaching, saying, "I am the living bread which came down from Heaven. If anyone eats of this bread, he will live forever; and the bread that I shall give is My flesh, which I shall give for the life of the world." John 6:51, A good number of those who heard those words of Jesus Christ that day became offended, and many in the crowd started quarreling among themselves, it is as if what was said to them by the great teacher was not acceptable. They would not mind being fed natural food by Him, for that would nourish their physical bodies, but when He started pointing them to eternal life, through His body, they seemed not willing to follow any more.

Amidst all of this, Jesus said something very revealing about the role of the Third Person of the Godhead – The Holy Spirit concerning our becoming

The Holy Spirit; the Third Person of the Godhead

'believers', for many were offended at His sayings and kind of drew back. Jesus clarified on His doctrine by saying this: "It is the Spirit who gives life; the flesh profits nothing. The words that I speak to you are spirit and they are life." John 6:63 Just reading as well as meditating on this verse you come to the conclusion that, for me and you to become believers; the Holy Spirit played a big role in enabling us to see Jesus as the true savior of our souls. The things of Heaven are spiritual. It takes the Deity of God, the Holy Spirit to draw us to the Savior. For us to even be able to see Jesus Christ as the truth, the way and the life, it takes divine intervention. Many look at Jesus as a great teacher; great prophet; very loving person; one who did unusual miracles, wonders and signs; as the one who gave us the Golden Rule 'do to others as you would like them to do to you,' but they are yet to see Him as well as receive Him as their personal Lord and Savior. Even some bow down as well as kneel at the mention of His name. Yet, they are to receive Him as their personal savior, and acknowledge Him to be their very loving friend who would die in our place so that we don't have to go to Hell!!!!!!!

Jesus continued to say that, one has to be born of the Spirit, "That which is born of the flesh is flesh, and that

The Holy Spirit, Baptizes Us into the Body of Christ

which is born of the Spirit is spirit." John 3:6   This is the first baptism; we are looking into it now; for it is very important for one to become a Child of God. It is the Holy Spirit of God that draws us to the Word of our Savior Jesus Christ, and when we yield to His guiding and leading, we end up receiving the Kingdom of God in the person of Jesus Christ. "For the Kingdom of God is not eating and drinking, but righteousness and peace and joy in the Holy Spirit." Rom 14:17

Jesus Christ went further and revealed to those people that day, who were in that audience; that they could not even come to Him unless they are drawn to Him by God Himself. "And He said, "Therefore, I have said to you that no one comes to Me unless it has been granted by My Father." John 6:65

The Danger of Blaspheming the Holy Spirit, as Far as Salvation is Concerned

The Bible says in St. Luke Chapter Twelve from verse one: "In the meantime, when an innumerable multitude of people had gathered together; So that they trampled one another. He began to say to His disciples, first of all, "Beware of the leaven of the Pharisees, which is hypocrisy." Luke 1:12 What I would like to

The Holy Spirit; the Third Person of the Godhead

bring to your attention is this phrase, 'Innumerable multitude,' for that lets you know that whatever Jesus was teaching that day could end up passed on to generations of people down the course of life. When you continue reading that chapter to verse ten, He says something about the Holy Spirit that is astounding. "Also I say to you, whoever confesses Me before men, him, the Son of Man also will confess before the angles of God, "But he who denies Me before men will be denied before the angels of God. "And anyone who speaks a word against the Son of Man, it will be forgiven him; but to him who blasphemes against the Holy Spirit, it will not be forgiven." Luke 12:10 When it came to the Holy Spirit, Jesus used very strong words in regard to the way the Third Person of the Godhead should be treated.

He is saying that when you reject the Holy Spirit as well as intentionally brush Him off, then your hope of salvation becomes zero; for it is Him who enables you to see Jesus Christ as Lord and Savior.

The two following scriptures indicate that truth. Jesus Christ said when they bring you to synagogues and authorities – of course to condemn you, as well as

The Holy Spirit, Baptizes Us into the Body of Christ

chastise you for being believers and witnesses. You should not worry about what you should answer, "For the Holy Spirit will teach you in that very hour what you ought to say." Luke 12:12

Beloved; The Holy Spirit, the third person of the Godhead: we need to know Him! That is what this book is all about. He is the one that draws us to Jesus Christ. By grace today, we are kings and priests of Almighty God, in a kingdom that will never pass away. "and has made us kings and priests to His God and Father, to Him be glory and dominion forever and ever. Amen." Rev 1:6 Because we yielded to the Holy Spirit's leading, when He showed us Christ; we allowed the Holy Spirit to Baptize us into the Body of Christ.

It is the Holy Spirit that Convicts Us of Sin

A human being was never created to live independent of God. God's glory was part of that, which would be in the lives of human beings, to their benefit for safety, peace, joy and righteousness. This holy presence of God was originally on the man and woman at the beginning of creation, before sin entered the human race. When Satan came to cause man to fall from grace; its suggestion to the woman, was to eat of

The Holy Spirit; the Third Person of the Godhead

the fruit that was in the midst of the Garden: the tempter told the human beings that they would be like God. The implication here is, you will not need God any more, you will be independent of God. Even though God had told man that the day they eat of the fruit of that tree of the Knowledge of Good and Evil they will surely die, "Then the serpent said to the woman, "You will not surely die. "For God knows that in the day you eat of it your eyes will be opened, and you will be like God, knowing good and evil." Gen 3:4-5

The Importance of Living by God's Word

Human beings were created, not to live by bread alone, but by every word that proceeds from the mouth of God." But He answered and said, "It is written, 'Man shall not live by bread alone, but by every word that proceeds from the mouth of God." Matt 4:4 Jesus said those words to the same tempter, that caused man and woman in the Garden of Eden to fall and sink in sin. The Glory of God lifted off man; man started depending on their corrupted judgement to live; death came in, wickedness had its way into the human race. Human beings could not even chase away one single demon through their own natural power; demons took control over mankind, we lost the dominion God gave us at creation through transgressing His commandments. Man dishonored God when he heeded the words of the enemy over God's command not to eat of that tree. That is why we need redemption.

We Needed a Savior

God saw all of that, and He decided to send us a Savior. The savior was to be the Second Person of the Godhead – Jesus Christ. The one to implement the Plan of Salvation was to be The Third Person of the Godhead, the Holy Spirit.

At Pilate's Judgement Seat, during the trial of Jesus Christ, in the Gospel of Matthew, Chapter Twenty-Seven, when Pilate asked the people what he should do between good and evil; the majority cried out, 'Crucify Him,' and give us the 'evil one.' They had sunken so low in sin, they could not tell the difference between good and evil. It seemed like they called good evil, and evil good. They asked for Barabbas the murder instead of Jesus the Savior.

Jesus said in the Gospel of Saint John Chapter Sixteen, Verse Eight, "And when He has come. He will

The Holy Spirit; the Third Person of the Godhead

convict the world of sin; and of righteousness; and of judgment: "of sin, because they do not believe in Me; "of righteousness, because I go to My Father and you see Me no more: "of judgment because the ruler of this world is judged." John 16:8-11 Man is in denial of their sinful condition, many reason that by educating man; giving man religion, would bring human beings out of evil and wicked acts. Incarcerations are on the rise in an effort to contain misguided behaviors of human beings. Drugs have been manufactured to suppress certain dangerous behaviors, all in an effort to tame mankind. Though all of this seems like a solution to man's dilemma but never addresses the core of the problem which is sin.

The remedy to sin is Jesus Christ; that is believing in the person of Christ and receiving Him as our Lord and Savior: that is the Heavenly prescription to man's dilemma. To really see, as well as receive Jesus Christ as our Savior, we need a guide, a helper. One who can divinely enable us to see the danger of rejecting God and provides us an opportunity to come to God, and that one is no other than the Third Person of the Godhead – The Holy Spirit. Thank God He is with us all, we only need to welcome Him into our lives.

The Holy Spirit, Baptizes Us into the Body of Christ

A Man Seemingly Opposed to Salvation through Jesus Christ, Ends Up Becoming a 'Born Again' Christian

There was a man that I knew in my course of pastoring, whose wife was born again, she was a lawyer by profession. This precious lady used to come and attend services at our church, she loved the Lord God Almighty, and she was full of faith and the Holy Spirit.

Her husband was yet to become a believer; in the sense of having received Jesus Christ as his personal Savior. This man seemed to be very opposed to things to do with salvation, he claimed that he was not a sinner, and he had a religion. He would say he was a good person – though his actions did not prove that. What is amazing, he started coming to our church services, claiming he came to see what was happening there. He would sit in the back of the church and watch; no clapping, no singing heavenly songs, just sitting there angry! He used to drink alcohol, go partying with his wife, but now his dear wife was no longer interested in that life style, for she had become born again. This man had tried everything to discourage his wife from staying saved, so that together they may continue that worldly

The Holy Spirit; the Third Person of the Godhead

lifestyle, but it did not work, for this wife of his, an attorney, took her salvation very dearly, and she loved the Word of God.

He could come to my office just to criticize his wife to me, as well as to talk bad things about Born Again people. To me, it seemed like something was convicting him of his sin and drawing him to the church supernaturally. He hated the Word of God, we preached, especially when we said that somebody needs to become Born Again; though strange enough, he kept coming! He would go back home and criticize everything that was in the sermon that day within his wife's hearing. This man was clear proof of what sin did to mankind, when man partook of the fruit of the Tree of the Knowledge of Good and Evil.

He Kept Coming

Despite all of that bitterness in him, whereby he seemed offended that his wife was no longer given to drinking alcohol, listening to ungodly music, hanging out with people full of themselves, he kept coming. His wife had placed her love and trust in God, which was completely opposite of his dreams for her, but he kept following her to church. He could argue that the reason why he was coming with her to church, was because he felt lonely.

The Man Responds to Salvation

This man, who was arguing that there are many ways that leads to God; he happened to come to church by himself on a certain day. It was a mid-day service; I was preaching about Hell. I let everybody know that Hell was not originally prepared for human beings, but demons, evil spirits and fallen angels: that God desires men to go to Heaven when life on earth is over. That the wages of sin is death; that God sent His only dear begotten son, Jesus Christ, to give us Heaven as well as an opportunity not to go to Hell.

That day, for some reason, that man received the message. He did not want to go to Hell, whereby he would never see his wife and children again. He raised his hands and said, he needed to become a 'Believer,' that day he gave his life to Jesus Christ and confessed Him to be his Lord and Savior, according to the scriptures. "That if you confess with your mouth the Lord Jesus and believe in your heart that God has raised Him from the dead, you will be saved. For with the heart one believes unto righteousness, and with the

The Holy Spirit; the Third Person of the Godhead

mouth confession is made unto salvation." Rom 9:9-10 This man said in his testimony that day that, that for some reason, something kept guiding him to our church. He said at first he did not want to be around Born Again people, for he felt condemned, but he had a supernatural conviction present in his heart that he needed to hear what they had to say.

I believe you and I, especially since you have been reading this book, we know where that conviction came from. The same one who convicts the world of sin and righteousness, and one who drew us to the well of salvation – Jesus Christ: that is the one who convicted that man of judgment and righteousness. The man escaped Hell Fire that day, for he responded to the leading of the Holy Spirit.

I later baptized that man and many others with him in the waters of Lake Victoria at Ggaba Beach, Kampala, Uganda, East Africa. It was a glorious day, I was standing in that lake with other ministers with water up to our chests. We Baptized twenty people that day. The Presence of God was tangible as I was baptizing. The power of God could be felt by all of us.

The Holy Spirit, Baptizes Us into the Body of Christ

You may be reading this book and you have never given your life to Jesus Christ as your Lord and Personal Savior, maybe you think that by just joining a church that will keep you out of Hell or you were told being a member of a religion would be the way for you to escape Hell fire. I would like to let you know, with all Godly love, that my brother, my sister, the gruesome death of the Son of God at the hands of vicious men can't be taken lightly. Just thinking about it lets you know that God means business. You either choose Heaven or you end up in Hell. God has no grandchildren. The Bible is very clear, "But as many as received Him, to them He gave the right to become children of God, to those who believe in His name:" John 1:12 Beloved, for you to become a child of God, you have to receive Jesus Christ as your personal savior. No one can do this for you; you can't say that I will go to Heaven because my father was a believer or my grandmother was a believer. It does not work that way. You have to receive Jesus Christ through your own will.

The Second Baptism

This baptism is done by 'Believers', the disciples of

The Holy Spirit; the Third Person of the Godhead

our Lord Jesus Christ. We are the ones that immerse people in water; the indication is, that we died with Christ and arose with Him, that our sins were washed away by the blood of Jesus Christ. We Believers were commissioned by our Lord Jesus Christ to Baptize those who have believed the Son of God, and have the life of God in them. It is as if Jesus Himself has given us the power of attorney to baptize in His stead, the Children of God. 'And Jesus came and spoke to them, saying, "All authority has been given to Me in heaven and on earth. "Go therefore and make disciples of all the nations baptizing them in the name of the Father and of the Son and of the Holy Spirit. "Teaching them to observe all things that I have commanded you: And lo, I am with you always, even to the end of the age." Amen." Matt 28:18-20

Always remember this: for you to baptize anyone into the Body of Christ, you only do it under delegated power; the authority in this matter is: Jesus Christ. The delegate is you, and you do it as if you are standing in the stead of Jesus Christ: to make it simple to understand, you do it in the Name of our Savior and Lord Jesus Christ.

The Holy Spirit, Baptizes Us into the Body of Christ

I have had opportunity to minister in different churches all over the world, they welcomed me very gladly, especially when they learned that I flow in the Gifts of the Holy Spirit, especially healing and deliverance. These precious pastors, bishops, apostles, reverends, ministers, brothers, sisters, doctors, archbishops, really desire the best for their congregations; they wanted God's people blessed.

In the process of doing this, I have run into situations whereby somebody could say, 'do we baptize in the Name of the Father, the Son and the Holy Spirit or do we baptize in the Name of Jesus.?' Some of the churches I preached in, they preferred to Baptize people in the Name of the Father, the Son and the Holy Spirit. Others insisted in baptizing in the Name of Jesus Christ. If you are not careful, this could become an issue of discord among them.

I have ministered in the Churches of God in Christ; Apostolic Churches; Methodist Churches; Episcopal Churches; Presbyterian Churches; Baptist Churches and Churches of Christ; Church of God; Full Gospel Churches; etc. and I have seen God touch people, heal them, set them free irrespective of the names written on the buildings. Beloved, many of you, it is very possible that you have been represented by an attorney in a legal

The Holy Spirit; the Third Person of the Godhead

Proceeding. when you go to court with that attorney, normally the attorney tells you that he will be representing you, when questions are asked in the court, it is not for you to answer to the court, but it is him to say what you have agreed on or what you have instructed him to accomplish. When that attorney argues your case, the Court is in full belief that whatever he or she is saying, is what you are saying. In fact, if you try to speak back to the judge instead of your attorney, the Court will ask you to be quiet, for you have already delegated your authority to that person.

Precious people of God, we chase away demons in the Name of Jesus Christ, we pray to God the Father in the Name of Jesus Christ, we preach the Gospel in the Name of Jesus Christ, those who say they baptize in the Name of the Father, the Son and the Holy Spirit in the Name of Jesus Christ they are right also, for Jesus said in the Gospel of Matthew, Chapter Twenty Eight, verse nineteen, "Go therefore and make disciples of all the nations, baptizing them in the name of the Father and of the Son and of the Holy Spirit." Matt 28:19 I really believe that our Lord Jesus Christ, wanted to introduce us believers to the Three Persons in the Godhead right at the time of baptism: The trinity, one God in three

The Holy Spirit, Baptizes Us into the Body of Christ

Persons; God the Father, God the Son, and God the Holy Spirit. In the book of Acts, Chapter Nineteen, Verse Two, our Brother Paul the Apostle asked the believers there whether they received the Holy Spirit when they believed. They said to him, "We have not so much as heard whether there is a Holy Spirit!" That should not be so. People need to know that there is a Holy Spirit. I met a very, very loving preacher in Nashville, Tennessee. This man of God and his wife, write and sing gospel songs. He told me and my wife that God gave him a good piece of property and he was able to make a big water body on it whereby he has been able to baptize a large number of people. He said to avoid confusion and conflict and unnecessary arguments, concerning Baptism, when he immerses people in the water, he says to them, "I baptize you in the Name of the Father, the Son and the Holy Spirit: in the Name of Jesus Christ."

He also said when they ask him, 'Why do you do this, this way?' He answers and says, "It would have been Jesus Christ Himself baptizing all of you, but He allowed me to stand in His shoes and baptize you." and He let me know that throughout His experience concerning Baptizing people, no one has been able to

The Holy Spirit; the Third Person of the Godhead

Disqualify the people that he has baptized from being true believers. I also let him know that my wife and I will never even think of disqualifying anybody who has been baptized by a disciple of Our Lord Jesus Christ from being a Child of God.!!!!!!!

Beloved There Is a Third Baptism

This one is when our Lord Jesus Christ Baptized you with the Holy Spirit and fire!!! John the Baptist bore witness to this when he was busy baptizing people with water in the Jordan River, "I indeed baptize you with water unto repentance, but He who is coming after me is mightier than I, whose sandals I am not worthy to carry. He will baptize you with the Holy Spirit and fire." Matt 3:11

As much as the first two baptisms are important; this one is very important for all believers. We all need this one, for through it we become equipped for the work of ministry; especially that we are supposed to be soul winners. I will deal with this one more later. Beloved, we need to work with the Holy Spirit.

The Holy Spirit, Baptizes Us into the Body of Christ

EL-OLAM

EVER-

LASTING

GOD

4

THE HELPER THE HOLY SPIRIT

OMUBEZI MWOYO MUTUKUVU

In Luganda Language

Uganda, Africa

"But when the Helper comes, whom I shall send to you from the Father, the Spirit of Truth, who proceeds from the Father; He will testify of Me." John 15:26

The Holy Spirit; the Third Person of the Godhead, we need His help and we need it urgently. We can't afford to do things apart from Him, for all our efforts to help others as well as ourselves without divine intervention of the Third Person of the Godhead, is futile. It is like driving a car without a lubricant; engine

The Holy Spirit; the Third Person of the Godhead

running without oil; it is like pulling a fish out of water and dumping it on land and while out of water, it seems completely helpless, though if you throw it back into the water, you witness the genius God put in it for that is where its help is. Precious people of God, our help is the Holy Spirit.

Helper in Prayer

The idea of prayer originated from God, it is the Lord God Almighty who invited man to communicate with Him through prayer. This venue is so powerful, that anybody, anywhere can change their circumstances through calling on God. Prayer enables us to understand that our God does hear, does care, does respond to our petitions and is involved in our day to day function, on earth.

Prayer takes away strife from among men and women, for it is a platform that is accessible to anybody willing to seek God. Prayer taps into the omnipotence of God and draws from the omniscience of the creator. By prayer, the omnipresence of God is acknowledged every day. The Lord God Almighty said in the book of Jeremiah, Chapter Thirty-three, verse three, "Call to Me, and I will answer you, and show you great and

The Helper: The Holy Spirit. Omubezi: Mwoyo Mutuvu

mighty things, which you do not know."Jer 33:3 There are many people today, who have given their lives to Jesus Christ as their personal savior, because of answered prayer.

Ten Men Become Converted through Prayer

I was preaching in a crusade, in Tulsa, Oklahoma, U.S.A. on the north side of that city. The Holy Spirit had impressed it on me that there was a need to conduct a crusade in that area. Therefore, we looked around for a place to carry out that crusade. I just stepped out through prayer by faith. When praying, the Lord God had enabled me to know that He will provide a venue, a tent as well as people to help me put this crusade together. This crusade was to cost at least $5,000 and it was to run for a week, I had to believe for everything and step out by faith.

What was so important in this Godly endeavor, was my willingness to let the Holy Spirit help me to help the People of God. I had a leading in my Spirit, it was an inner witness; it was a very strong conviction that I had to talk to the pastor of a certain church in that area. This church owned a good piece of property with an open field where we could pitch a tent that could seat at least

The Holy Spirit; the Third Person of the Godhead

two hundred and fifty people. I went and met this pastor for the first time, we talked and prayed together in regard to this matter. Well, after one week, he called me back saying that he believes it is God's will for me to do that crusade in that area, this was during the summer. The will of God is alive and powerful, it is the Word of God spoken to our inner person; when God speaks to you, concerning anything, His be clearly recognized by you. "For the word of God is living and powerful, and sharper than any two-edged sword, piercing even to the division of soul and spirit, and of joints and marrow, and is a discerner of the thoughts and intents of the heart." Heb. 4:12

Never be worried about knowing God's will when you pray; the Helper, the Holy Spirit will always help you to know the direction to take. Many times it is through the inner witness: it is a divine knowing that something good is going to happen to you in regard to your prayers; it's a revelation of what needs to be done to arrive to the manifestation of the answer. You do not have to be anxious, "Be anxious for nothing but in everything by prayer and supplication, with thanksgiving, let your request be made known to God

The Helper: The Holy Spirit. Omubezi: Mwoyo Mutuvu

and the peace of God, which surpasses all understanding, will guard your hearts and minds through Christ Jesus." Phil 4:6-7 When I stepped out in prayer to have that crusade done in that area of the country of the United States of America, the only real help I had was the Holy Spirit of God. I had to believe that others would be able to hear the voice of God for themselves, so that they may participate. Precious one, the Third Person of the Godhead can cause as well as help people hear God's voice in regard to what God wants done.

I needed money to make the crusade happen, all that I had in my possession cash wise was $100.00. As I continued praying to God for the provision of money, I suddenly had a strong inner witness, a knowing that I needed to go and meet those in charge of the Evangelical Outreach of a big episcopal church in Tulsa, Oklahoma.

I did meet with the men's group during one of their prayer sessions, and I shared with them what God had put on my heart; what was so amazing, these 'Believers' said, they had been talking about the possibility of carrying out evangelism in that area, and they believe

The Holy Spirit; the Third Person of the Godhead

I am an answer to their prayers! They said they will get poles and stalks made for my tent. I had a tent that sits two hundred and fifty people, that was given to me by an evangelist from Oklahoma City, it was only the big outside top covering, which I had; the topline, but it lacked the poles and stalks to make it stand. The men of that church gave me $5,000.00 to help me with the crusade. Poles were made for the tent, a platform was built on the venue, chairs were made available, a rental was obtained and we were also able to have security at the crusade ground. All of this was made possible because of the help of the Holy Spirit in prayer.

The Holy Spirit, Helper in Prayer

We continued to pray, for we needed various choirs and co-preachers during the crusade. As you are aware, I am a man on a mission from Uganda, Africa assigned by God to carry out world evangelism in the United States of America. Even as I write this book, I and my wife, Dr. Gail Kayiwa, are both lead pastors of 'World Evangelism Healing Worship Center' in the great City of Chicago, Illinois, U.S.A. Always, the Lord God lets me know that I have to work with the American ministers, in order to be effective. That is why I was led by the Holy Spirit to invite a number of churches in

The Helper: The Holy Spirit. Omubezi: Mwoyo Mutukuvu

Oklahoma to participate in that crusade; churches of 'Believers,': those who believe that Jesus Christ saves, heals, delivers, and gives abundant life.

Seven Churches Get Involved Instantly

Seven churches in Oklahoma became involved. These were congregations with different names: a Baptist Church in the City of Tulsa. a Methodist Church out in the country in one of the towns on the South Side of Tulsa; a Pentecostal Church in Oklahoma City – U.S.A.; African Methodist Episcopal Church on the North side of the City of Tulsa; The House of Prayer Church in North Tulsa; a Baptist Church in downtown Tulsa and the Episcopal Church that helped me with the tent.

I received food supplies from the food bank at Oral Roberts University, all of this happened as answered prayer through the help of the Holy Spirit. Five thousand very nice flyers were made with four big banners that were displayed at the tent ground: inscribed on, 'God loves you and sent His son to die for you.' That, 'Jesus is Lord.' Another one read: 'It is God's will for you to become born again.' This is how

The Holy Spirit; the Third Person of the Godhead

the preaching went, I would let an American pastor from one of those churches preach for thirty minutes and I would follow in the next hour, then we would pray for people to receive miracles, wonders and signs. There was a day when the power of God was so present, that everybody could say, surely the presence of the Lord is in this place. That day the place was full of people, the two hundred chairs inside the tent were already occupied. In addition, about one hundred people were standing around the tent, it was a Saturday evening; all kinds of people were there. Just looking at that congregation, which was diverse, would make one easily acknowledge, that Jesus was among us. You could feel the love of God.

I would be praying for the people, and the power of God would come upon them tangibly. I would ask them to come forward, hold one another's hands, and I would ask about seven to twelve people to come and stand in front of the pulpit, and hold their hands together while facing me. I had ushers standing behind them, then I would tell them that I was going to pray for them to receive the supernatural touch of God's tangible power, and every time I did that, that power would come on them and literally sweep them off their feet, this could

The Helper; The Holy Spirit. Omubezi: Mwoyo Mutukuvu

cause the whole audience to go into an uproar as well as loudly give glory to the Lord God Almighty.

Ten Yet to Get Born Again Men Step Forth for Prayer

I asked for ten men, present on that crusade ground, who have never accepted Jesus Christ as their personal Savior, to come forth and hold hands tightly together as I pray for them to experience the power of God.

They did come forth! They hurried to the front, they were very curious and wanted to know if that power was real for they had seen people falling backwards on their backs as I prayed for them in the Name of Jesus Christ. You could sense how curious these men were when they came forth; I was standing about two meters from them and I suddenly said, 'touch the power of God in the Name of Jesus Christ of Nazareth.' These men shook under the power of God, it was like a live electrical current going through their bodies.

Their bodies vibrated under that power, they did not even know how they ended up on their backs on the floor. I asked them whether they wanted to receive Jesus Christ as their personal Savior, they gladly said, 'yes.' I also went ahead and prayed for them to receive the Baptism of the Holy Spirit with evidence of speaking in tongues, which happened. They gladly received the infilling of the Holy Spirit. and spoke in a

The Holy Spirit; the Third Person of the Godhead

Heavenly language. What people saw that day was answered prayer. That led them to desire to come forth and be prayed for as well. We saw amazing healing miracles manifest right there before all of us, the faith of many was boosted and a number of them came to the podium and gave amazing testimonies.

Helper with Prayer – The Holy Spirit

Prayer was not necessarily meant to tell God, what He does not know, for if that was the case, there would be little difference between the creator and the creation. We are not particularly heard because of so many words we say, "And when you pray, do not use vain repetitions as the heathen do, For they think that they will be heard for their many words. "Therefore, do not be like them. For your Father knows the things you have need of before you ask Him." Matt 6:8

The Bible admonishes us to pray with all prayer and supplication in the Spirit. "Praying always with all prayers and supplication in the Spirit, being watchful to this end with all perseverance and supplication for all the saints." Eph 6:18 The word 'Spirit used in that verse has a capital 'S' designating the Holy Spirit, not the spirit of a human being; implying that the Holy Spirit would be a present help in our prayers.

The Helper: The Holy Spirit. Omubezi: Mwoyo Mutukuvu

Every time one engages prayer, it means either they are responding to the witness of the Holy Spirit in their hearts or they are acting in the authority given to them by Jesus Christ for asserting God's will in any circumstances. In that aspect, they could be asking for something from God, or using what they have already been given to bring forth a change. Prayer, other times can just be communication with God through praise, worship and adoration.

Abraham Intercedes for Sodom and Gomorrah

In Genesis Chapter Eighteen, the Lord appeared to Abraham, after he ministered to the Lord. The Lord decided to reveal to him what that mission was about, Abraham had fellowshipped with the LORD, and in the process the Lord God said this: "And the Lord said, "Shall I hide from Abraham what I am doing. "since Abraham shall surely become a great and mighty nation, and all nations of the earth shall be blessed in him?" Gen 18:17-18 Every time we call on God in prayer, is an act of faith, I am talking about prayer that is faith under guarded; an act that acknowledges that God hears us when we call upon Him. God sees our faith and in the process, the Holy Spirit sheds light on

The Holy Spirit; the Third Person of the Godhead

how we ought to pray. It is very interesting in the Book of Genesis, that when Abraham received the revelation from God that judgment was about to strike the people in those cities, that Abraham started right away to intercede for them; it was as if divine compassion came upon him.

His Intercession was Based on God's Will

Abraham was helped by the Spirit of Truth, the Holy Spirit, to present his prayers on grounds of righteousness, that God was a righteous judge, and would spare a nation, city, neighborhood because of the existence of God fearing and God honoring people in that region. His petition to God seems to be very strong, he knew something about what pleases God. He did not just go into vain repetitions but based his intersession on that which the Lord God would consider in order to spare the cities of Sodom and Gomorrah. This is in line with the book of First John, Chapter Five Verse Fourteen: "Now this is the confidence that we have in Him, that if we ask anything according to His will, He hears us. And if we know that He hears us, whatever we ask, we know that we have the petition that we have asked of Him." I John 5:14-15

The Helper: The Holy Spirit. Omubezi: Mwoyo Mutukuvu

Abraham was very effective in his prayer that day, God was responding to him. God loves answering our prayers, that is why the Third Person of the Godhead – the Holy Spirit helps us to know God's will through His already written Word – the Holy Bible, that we could base our prayers on God's promises, for faith begins where God's will, is known.

The Holy Bible was written, under the inspiration and guidance of the Holy Spirit; the scriptures, are for exhortation, edification, correction, instruction, "All scripture is given by inspiration of God, and is profitable for doctrine, for reproof, for correction, for instruction in righteousness, that the man of God may be complete, thoroughly equipped for every good work." 2Tim 3:16-17

Prayer based on God's word is very effective, this kind of function is truly a result of a life yielded to the Holy Spirit; one tends to connect into God's will divinely. You pray in the compassion of the Lord Jesus Christ, you tend to have a redemptive approach with a bigger picture of the circumstances, that God is not just trying to have you have something good, but He is also setting you up to become a channel of blessings. "Where do wars and fights come from among you? Do they not come from your desires for pleasure that war in your members? You lust and do not have. You murder and covet and cannot obtain. You fight and war. Yet you do not have because you do not ask. You ask and do not receive, because you ask amiss, that you may spend it on your pleasures." James 4:1-3

learning from Solomon's Answered Prayer

In the Book of First Kings Chapter Three, the Bible introduces us to a young man by the name of Solomon, he was a son to King David, and had inherited his father's throne through the will of God. Solomon was young and inexperienced in governing. He needed help. He was amidst God's people, and wanted to do right; he was a king.

You are a king as well

According to the Holy Bible, in case you received Jesus Christ as your personal savior and became a new person in Him; you definitely became a king and a priest. "and has made us kings and priests to His God and Father, to Him be glory and dominion forever and ever. Amen." Rev 1:6 Your position on earth, you as a believer, is a kingly one, you are meant to execute God's will on the earth, like Solomon, there is a lot for

The Helper: The Holy Spirit. Omubezy: Mwoyo Mutukuvu

you to accomplish through prayer for the redemption of mankind. There are some resources; you need to have as a soul winner.

Solomon example continued: -

Solomon loved the Lord, and offered a lot of burnt offerings to Him; a thousand. God appeared to him at night in a vision, "At Gibeon the LORD appeared to Solomon in a dream at night, and God said, "Ask What shall I give you?" 1 Kin 3:5 This lines up very well with the desire of God to answer prayers. When the Second Person of the Godhead, Jesus Christ came on earth and put on flesh, He gave us similar offer, "Ask! and it will be given to you; seek, and you will find, knock and it will be opened to you." Matt 7:7 This puts us, we believers and Solomon on the same platform of grace – we can ask for anything.

Solomon Asks

Solomon responded to God's offer and asked for an understanding heart to Judge God's people. "Therefore give to your servant an understanding heart, to Judge your people that I may discern between good and evil. For who is able to Judge this great people of yours?" I Kin 3:9 It is so profound that Solomon prayed that way, this young man must have been helped, for him to have

The Holy Spirit; the Third Person of the Godhead

a bigger picture of the purpose of prayer. Precious one, God answers prayer. God responded to this request right away, the word of God says, "The speech pleased the Lord, that Solomon had asked this thing. Then God said to him: "Because you have asked this thing, and have not asked long life for yourself, nor have asked riches for yourself, nor have asked the life of your enemies, but have asked for yourself understanding to discern justice, "behold I have done according to your words; see, I have given you a wise and understanding heart, so that there has not been anyone like you before you, nor, shall any like you arise after you. "And I have also given you what you have not asked: both riches and honor, so that there shall not be anyone like you among the kings of all your days." I Kin 3:10-13 Wow, this is amazing!!!

The purpose of this book

This book is about the Holy Spirit, the Third Person of the Godhead. One we really have to be intimate with, for He is the gateway to the supernatural things of God. We want God's power in our lives, and churches; we want to see things like: people healed of all diseases in the Name of Jesus Christ; demons leaving places and territories when we command them to go in the Name

The Helper: The Holy Spirit. Omubezi; Mwoyo Mutukuvu

of Jesus Christ; we want to witness creative miracles; we need the wisdom and knowledge of God; we desire to experience the anointing of God that destroys addictions, oppressions and bad habits. We know that all of those things exist in God. We don't want to be in a situation where we lay hands on the sick and nothing happens! Tell the devils to leave, and they just sit there and stare at us! Pronounce a blessing and nothing happens! We need preachers who are truly anointed by the Lord God Almighty, and disciples who have some power. "Thus says the LORD: 'Heaven is My throne, And earth is My footstool. Where is the house that you will build Me? And where is the place of My rest? For all those things My hands have made, And all those things exist," Says the LORD. "But on this one will I look: On him who is poor and of a contrite spirit, And who trembles at My word." Is. 66:1-2

GOLDEN RULE NUMBER 3

Your willingness to share, apply, to work, let flow, implement, exercise, communicate, explain, proclaim, engage, through what you are asking God for; will determine the extent of the supply of that grace.

The Holy Spirit; the Third Person of the Godhead

The widow in Second Kings Chapter Four, of the wives of the Sons of the Prophets, was instructed to collect as many vessels as she could; the supernatural supply of oil flowed into all the vessels she was willing to present. The oil stopped at the last vessel! Then, she went ahead and paid off the debt and kept the rest of the finances for the family.

Willingness to be a Blessing

Solomon was willing to apply the wisdom he asked for, from God to administer justice, and God gave it to him.

When you talk to God about power, miracles, wonders and signs, you have to be willing to utilize those graces for the good of all. Those graces are supposed to point people to God; to Jesus Christ, the Savior, to bring people to a Spirit filled life: they are not just for self-gratification. They are for a cause bigger than us. No wonder the Word, 'yourself' is repeated three times in I Kings 3:11 to help you make a difference between the narrow way and the broad way.

Child of God, it is time for miracles, wonders, and signs to flow! You should be able to lay hands on the sick, and they recover. You should be able to speak in

The Helper: The Holy Spirit. Omubezi: Mwoyo Mutukuvu

You should be able to speak in heavenly languages – tongues, you should be able to be gracious to people, you should be able to chase away a demon in the Name of Jesus Christ. The time for playing games is over. We are dealing with real challenges and we need the provisions of God almighty to prevail. We are caught up in a spiritual warfare whereby we cannot excuse ourselves. All what I am writing, I am being led by the Holy Spirit; He has my pen, I am a co-worker with the Lord: God has sent me to you with these words of power and love.

Satan Cannot Hold Away God's Power

Devils and demons cannot hold away God's power from flowing through you. They cannot even touch the anointing, for it is disastrous to them. The power of God is like fire towards them, it burns them out. I have witnessed this a number of times, where I have ministered with the power of God present and I have heard demons cry out loudly that the fire of God is burning them up. There is something about the anointing that causes these evil spirits to lose control as well as the ability to function. The power of God hits them so hard, and knocks them unconscious. The power of God unseats devils and drives them out.

The Holy Spirit; the Third Person of the Godhead

We Christians, having the power of God in our lives, is not an option, it's a must. Powerlessness and confusion of mind should not be at all the nature of a believer. We have to be strong, we have to operate in dominion and the only way to do this is to rely on the helper, the Holy Spirit.

A Man Delivered, as demons Cry Out loudly: that God's fire is Burning Them Up

I was teaching in a church in Tulsa, Oklahoma, U.S.A., it was a big one, and a lot of people were seated out there in the pews, a Bishop of a very big denomination invited me to teach. This Bishop was over about 60 churches in that area. The people in the church were very well dressed, the service had started at 7:00pm. The Holy Spirit had instructed me through inner witness to teach and minister the Word of God about resurrection power: The power that raised Jesus Christ from the dead.

Man Falls Off the Pew

When I started proclaiming that: No demonic power can stop the resurrection power of God from flowing, a

The Helper: The Holy Spirit. Omubezi: Mwoyo Mutukuzu

Man about eight meters from the pulpit where I was standing, shook violently and fell off the pew. He was a huge and well-dressed man. Those around him were perplexed, everyone turned and looked intently to figure out what was happening. Well, I knew that deliverance was taking place right there, so I continued proclaiming that the power of God is like fire to the demonic. The moment I said that, those devils started crying aloud that the fire of God was burning them up!

Beloved of God, those spirits that had taken abode in that man's life were crying out for help and none of us was willing to help them. They were burning. I went further and said, 'Let the fire of God burn you up: I cast you out of that man in the Name of Jesus Christ of Nazareth, right now.' They convulsed the man's body and cried their last cry, loudly, and they were no more.

The man lay down on the ground for some time; when he came to himself, he was very surprised that he was laying down on the carpet, he wondered what happened. I told him what took place. He stood to his feet and started giving glory to God loudly. He said he had been struggling with sexual addiction, that he had

The Holy Spirit; the Third Person of the Godhead

been watching bad things on the internet; it was so bad, that though he was married, he would be lusting at every woman who passed by him. It was as if certain devils had taken control of him. He said the only thing he remembers unusual that day, in that service, is when I walked in to preach; when the Bishop of that church handed me the microphone; that something commanded him to leave as quickly as possible! Something was telling him to leave the service, but for some reason he lacked the strength to get up and leave, so he tarried on, for his wife and children were in the service as well.

He went ahead and said; 'time came when I was as if going in circles, like the power of God was unbinding me.'

This man was set free by God's power, and he left a rejuvenated human being, restored through the redemptive power of our Lord Jesus Christ: set free and finally renewed for God's glory. This deliverance is one of the many I have witnessed while ministering. Devils are there and they can hide in human bodies and mess-up lives. It takes the power of the Holy Spirit to

The Helper: The Holy Spirit. Omubezi; Mwoyo Mutukuvu

Punish them as well as bring healing to the area in the human body where they have inflicted pain and suffering as well as caused malfunction.

Your willingness to let the power of God flow through you will determine the level of availability of that grace.

It is your willingness to do what God asks of you that determines the flow of the provision of all the resources you need, everything you need, God has it: He has the money, the buildings, the vehicles, the planes, the yachts, the boats…etc. But, you have to be willing to live the life that puts the Kingdom of God first, "But seek first the Kingdom of God and His righteousness, and all these things shall be added to you." Matt 6:33 You have to be desire to use what you ask of the Lord to the betterment of humanity.

Having so much stuff, without the compassion to share it, is not healthy and is not heavenly. Life down here on earth ends, you and I know very well that we are only stewards of God's money, buildings, land, farms, vehicles, minerals, etc., for the earth is the Lord's and its fullness, "The earth is the LORD's and all its

The Holy Spirit; the Third Person of the Godhead

fullness, The world and those who dwell therein. For He has founded it upon the seas, And established it upon the waters." Ps 24:1-2 Yes, you have your name on that title; the bank account is in your name; but the real truth is, the money belongs to God. For the Word of God says, "The silver is Mine, and the gold is Mine, says the LORD of hosts." Hag 2:8 It is His, and the Helper; The Holy Spirit – the Third Person of the Godhead is helping us right now through this book to become helpers as well.

You are blessed by God to become a blessing, you are empowered by God to empower others, you are encouraged to encourage, strengthened to strengthen, taught to teach, that is what disciples do. The peace you have been given by God is for you to share with others; that joy in your life blesses someone, you are the light of the world and the salt to the world; you season circumstances and situation with a heavenly aroma.

You are a walking, speaking, worthy to behold miracle of the Lord God; the Fruits of the Holy Spirit are in you for the benefit of many. There are Gifts of the Holy Spirit in your life that are meant to profit all. "But the manifestation of the Spirit is given to each one for the profit of all." 1 Cor 12:7

The Helper: The Holy Spirit. Omubezi: Mwoyo Mutukuvu

Holy Spirit – Helper in Prayer Continued

All of us want to offer effective prayers for that is the venue of communication God Almighty provided us. The idea of prayer was God initiated. In his Omniscience, He graciously gave us a say in His creative work. Prayer was never intended to tell God What He did not know; God knows everything that is happening: it was not designed to just command God to do things for us. There are various things that can be accomplished through prayer. For example, one gets edified when they pray, that is you get built up spiritually; become divinely strengthened and equipped to do good works. "But you, beloved, building yourself up on your most holy faith, praying in the Holy Spirit." Jude 20

Praying in the Holy Spirit: -

Glory to God, as you and I continue on this amazing journey of revelation knowledge, concerning the help of the Holy Spirit in prayer, this is something very important for us to examine. I am a born again, 'Spirit filled' child of God, I do pray in the Holy Spirit. I have been able to pray in the Holy Spirit since 1985. When

The Holy Spirit; the Third Person of the Godhead

I received the Baptism of the Holy Spirit, with evidence of speaking in tongues. This help which I obtained through obeying as well as seeking the Word of God concerning help in prayer, has sustained me through very tough challenges; I mean situations whereby I did not know what to pray for. "Likewise, the Spirit also helps in our weaknesses. For we do not know what we should pray for as we ought, but the Spirit Himself makes intercession for us with groanings which cannot be uttered. Now He who searches the hearts knows what the mind of the Spirit is, because He makes intercession for the Saints according to the will of God." Rom 8:26-27

The Baptism of the Holy Spirit

For you to pray in the Holy Spirit, you need to have been baptized in the Holy Spirit, this is what I refer to as the Third Baptism for a believer.

This baptism, is when our Lord Jesus Christ immerses you in the Holy Spirit; that is when you get infilled by the presence of the Holy Spirit: the Holy Spirit in you, and the Holy Spirit upon you. John testified to this when he was busy baptizing people at the Jordan River. "I indeed baptize you with water unto

The Helper: The Holy Spirit. Omubezi: Mwoyo Mutukuvu

repentance, but He who is coming after me is mightier than I, whose sandals I am not worthy to carry. He will baptize you with the Holy Spirit and fire." Matt 3:11 This baptism is for all willing believers; it is during this holy event that you receive a divine prayer language – a supernatural help in prayer.

Praying in Tongues

One of the results of being baptized in the Holy Spirit and Fire, is the ability to speak in a heavenly language, referred to as tongues. In the book of Acts Chapter Ten, when Cornelius a centurion of the Roman Regiment, a Gentile, who happened to love God and prayed to Him continuously, had a visitation of an Angel of God, whereby he was given instructions to send for a disciple of the Lord Jesus Christ, called Peter. This was a time of transition from the Old Testament to the New Testament, from the old covenant rituals, to the new covenant ministerial of righteousness: All odds were against Cornelius because of the conflicting old way of looking at and conducting religious ceremonies verses the new way of grace, which Jesus had ushered in, whereby a religious Jew would not even go to the house of the gentile, to sit down and eat with them! But

The Holy Spirit – The Third Person of the Godhead

something very remarkable took place in that man's house, that helped the apostles to reexamine themselves and look at things differently in regard to salvation.

People in Cornelius' House Receive a Heavenly Prayer Language

The Bible says, that when Peter came to the house of Cornelius, a Gentile, that while he was still preaching the Gospel of Grace; that Gospel – Good News, that Jesus Christ is the Son of the Living God; came on earth and was born by a virgin woman – Mary; taught and preached the kingdom of God with signs and wonders accompanying his words, that He died for sinners on the cross and rose again from the dead after three days, that He is alive today and is as well seated at the Right Hand of God making intercession for us. "To Him all the people witnessed that, through His Name, whoever believes in Him will receive remission of sins." While Peter was still speaking these words, the Holy Spirit fell upon all who heard the word. And those of the circumcision who believed were astonished, as many as came with Peter, because the Gift of the Holy Spirit had been poured out on the Gentiles also. For they heard them speak with tongues, and magnify God. Then Peter answered, "Can anyone forbid water that this should not

The Helper: The Holy Spirit. Omubezi: Mwoyo Mutukuvu

be baptized, who have received the Holy Spirit, just as we have?" Acts 10:43-47 Saint Paul spoke in tongues, he bears witness to the same in the book of First Corinthians, "I thank my God I speak with tongues more than you all." I Cor 14:18

Saint Jude spoke in tongues, that is why he admonishes us to pray in the Holy Spirit, "But you beloved, building yourselves up on your most Holy Faith, praying in the Holy Spirit." Jude 1:20

Saint Mary, the mother of Jesus Christ, prayed in tongues as well, for she was part of those who were in the upper room waiting on the promise of the Father – the Holy Spirit. "When the Day of Pentecost had fully come, they were all with one accord in one place. And suddenly there came a sound from Heaven, as of a rushing mighty wind, and it filled the whole house where they were sitting. Then there appeared to them divided tongues, as of fire, and one sat upon each of them. And they were all filled with the Holy Spirit and began to speak with other tongues, as the Holy Spirit gave them utterance." Acts 2:1-4

The twelve men, disciples; believers in our Lord Jesus Christ, whom Paul came across at Ephesus, whom he baptized in water, in the Name of Our Lord Jesus

The Holy Spirit; the Third Person of the Godhead

Christ spoke in tongues. These men who were yet to know whether there was the Holy Spirit; for the Bible says, When Paul laid his hands on them to receive the Baptism of the Holy Spirit, with evidence of speaking in tongues, that something amazing happened, "And when Paul had laid hands on them, the Holy Spirit came upon them, and they spoke with tongues and prophesied." Acts 19:6 They received a prayer language – tongues.

We All Need the Help of the Holy Spirit in Prayer

You notice through reading this book, that God Almighty has moved me to look into this grace, very keenly with you, concerning help in prayer through speaking in tongues. This is not a gift for just a few; No, No! It is for who so ever is willing to be helped by the Third Person of the Godhead – the Holy Spirit. In fact, the Bible says that these signs follow those who believe. "And these signs will follow those who believe: In My name they will cast out demons; they will speak with new tongues." Mark 16:17

You are supposed to pray in tongues, you can pray in those heavenly tongues; you just need to be willing. "He who speaks in a tongue edifies himself, but he who

The Helper: The Holy Spirit. Omubezi: Mwoyo Mutukuvu

prophesies edifies the church." I Cor 14:4 When you pray in tongues, you are speaking mysteries, "For he who speaks in a tongue does not speak to men but to God, for no one understands him; however, in the Spirit he speaks mysteries." I Cor14:2 As I write this book, we have a church on the South Side of Chicago, in a place where there have been quite a few murders. Chicago is a great city, very modern and with so many businesses and wonderful buildings. Its suburbs are amazing, filled with hard working people and many who mind their own business. But, this particular area has seen gun violence in an unusual measure, and God Almighty sent us there to minister. The police have tried their best to deter crime in that area, but the criminals seem to just continue to have their way. It is very, very obvious that there must be a way to come to the core of this matter; that is to root out the problem. We know what that is, the real killer is the devil, and for that reason, we are willing as a church to use every help available from God to help the people in that area.

The good news is we have believers who are filled with the Holy Spirit, and empowered to pray in tongues, to help change the tide, and it is working. These believers pray in the Spirit every week, right in the City of Chicago, trusting The Holy Spirit to give them the words to resolve the mystery of murder in that area. You might be dealing with a situation which is so dire that you don't know where to begin to resolve it. Precious one, you need the help of the Holy Spirit, now, you need divine intervention. That is why you need a prayer language.

Ask and It Shall Be Given

This grace is received through asking. You have to seek, knock, that is you go after that help from God; you don't shy away from this heavenly gift because of erroneous teaching by some who need help from the Holy Spirit themselves. Don't let anybody tell you that you do not need this help. "but exhort one another, daily while it is called "today," lest any of you be hardened though the deceitfulness of sin." Heb. 3:13 This script is in your hands, by the leading of the Holy Spirit, for He is helping you to tap into the very needed help in regard to prayer.

The Holy Spirit is a very present help to all of us, God's children, anywhere in the world, regardless of denomination limitations; we are not those labels put on us by man: we are God's children, first and foremost. "Beware lest anyone cheat you through philosophy and empty deceit, according to the traditions of men, accor-

The Helper: The Holy Spirit. Omubezi: Mwoyo Mutukuvu

ding to the basic principles of the world, and not according to Christ. For in Him dwells all the fullness of the Godhead bodily." Col 2:8-9

Ask Jesus Christ to Baptize You with the Holy Spirit, with Evidence of Speaking in Tongues, Please, and Do It Right Now

I Pray for Twenty People and They Receive the Baptism of the Holy Spirit, with Evidence of Speaking in Tongues, Instantly

It was a Sunday morning, during those days when I would be invited by various churches in Uganda, Africa to minister the power filled Gospel of our Lord and Savior Jesus Christ. This particular incident happened in a church in the City of Entebbe, Uganda. That morning the service began with praise and dance for the Lord, songs were sung that are gospel centered; songs that declares who we are in Christ; songs that praised God for what He has done for us. In the Country of Uganda, there are very powerful songs that have been birthed through the church in the Luganda language with musical beats that are amazing! You can't just sit

The Holy Spirit; the Third Person of the Godhead

there and do nothing, you end up rising up and dancing for the Lord God, with all your might, when these songs are played by those born again believers. Well, I danced and praised the Lord with the saints, then suddenly, they switched to worship; that is vertical expression of adoration of God through words that are focused on who God is. That went on for thirty minutes, then I felt the Holy Presence of the Holy Spirit all over the sanctuary, it was as if God was smiling on us; then I spoke to the Pastor who had invited me, asking him to let me have the microphone right away so that I could start ministering to the people.

The Lord Jesus Christ spoke to me through an inner witness to call out those who needed a divine prayer language by the Holy Spirit of God. I explained to them what I meant, through scriptures, I let them know that this promise was for them and their children, "For the promise is to you and your children, and to all who are afar off, as many as the Lord our God will call." Acts 2:39 That is the promise of the baptism of the Holy Spirit, with evidence of speaking in tongues.

Twenty Men Come Forth to Receive

Quickly, without any delay, twenty very highly motivated men stepped to the front with their hearts full

The Helper: The Holy Spirit. Omubezi: Mwoyo Mutukuvu

of faith, ready to receive. I asked them to lift their holy hands towards heaven, then I said, 'Receive the Baptism of the Holy Spirit with evidence of speaking in tongues from our Lord and Savior Jesus Christ, the Lord.' Before I completed the sentence, those people were filled with the Holy Spirit and they spoke in tongues for the next ten minutes, non-stop. It was so glorious; these people were filled with joy unspeakable. Healing broke out in that church that day, there was heavenly rejoicing; indeed, we all could say that surely we had been with the LORD.

In case you have never received the Baptism of the Holy Spirit with evidence of speaking in tongues; I would like to pray for you right now: -

'Receive the Baptism of the Holy Spirit with the evidence of speaking in tongues, right now, in the Name of Jesus Christ.' Jesus Christ is baptizing you with the Holy Spirit right now, receive the Holy Spirit with His power, receive now in the Name of Jesus Christ.

Something else I would like you to know is that these tongues are not from your head, these are words which are given to you supernaturally, right to your tongue, and you just speak them by faith; the more you speak the more words are given to you, for the Holy

The Holy Spirit; the Third Person of the Godhead

Spirit gives you utterance. Find a church were they do not preach against this grace, an assembly of believes, not doubters. People who can inspire you to grow in what you have received; people who rejoice at God's promises, a church with a sound doctrine, where people rejoice in the Lord. "Rejoice always, pray without ceasing, in everything give thanks; for this is the will of God in Christ Jesus for you. Do not quench the Spirit. Do not despise prophesies." 2Thl 5:16-20 We all need this help – praying in tongues.

The Holy Spirit

In Romans, Chapter Eight, verse nine, He is referred to as the Spirit of Christ, indicating that the Third Person of the Godhead is one with Christ; the scripture further calls the Holy Spirit, The Spirit of God, hereby asserting that He is one with God the Father. "But you are not in the flesh but in the Spirit, if indeed the Spirit of God dwells in you. Now if any one does not have the Spirit of Christ, he is not His." Rom 8:9

The Spirit of God

At the beginning of creation, in Genesis Chapter One

The Helper: The Holy Spirit. Omubezi: Mwoyo Mutukuvu

we get a glimpse of the Third Person of the Godhead's presence; He was hovering over the face of the water. The Bible tells us that the earth was without form and void, and darkness was on the face of the deep, but within that circumstance, was a Helper; a creator; one with God the Father and God the Son; The Holy Spirit. He is being introduced to us so early in the scriptures, for we are supposed to know Him. "The earth was without form, and void; and darkness was on the face of the deep. And the Spirit of God was hovering over the face of the waters. Then God said, "Let there be light"; and there was light." Gen 1:2-3

I am a witness to that kind of presence, there are a number of times when I am ministering and suddenly I sense a Holy Presence of God; the Holy Spirit, and in those services there would be a need for divine intervention regarding various challenges: need for healing, need for financial breakthrough, need for deliverance, need for direction about an important life decision, and the moment I start speaking healing and deliverance, as well as miracles, wonders and signs, according to the Holy Word of God, by the leading of the Holy Spirit, in the Name of Jesus Christ, those dire situations get turned around.

People become healed, delivered, obtain breakthrough

The Holy Spirit; the Third Person of the Godhead

in their finances, they receive divine power and wisdom to handle various challenges, yokes are broken and burdens are removed; void and darkness are dispelled, light fills people's lives. Thanks for the Spirit of God; the Holy Spirit. God the Father spoke, and the Holy Spirit manifested what was spoken, "Let there be light" and there was light.

The Spirit of Wisdom and Understanding

Precious one, we need wisdom, you need God's wisdom, for it seems like there are many solutions; many roads; many offers; many suggestions about life that are thrown and presented to us today. Always remember, everything that glitters is not gold. Man fell in the Garden of Eden, through a very cunning offer from the enemy of our soul, Satan.

The temptation was; you will not need God, for when you eat of the fruit of the tree of the knowledge of good and evil, you will become like Him. "Then the serpent said to the woman, "You will not surely die. For God knows that in the day you eat of it your eyes will be opened, and you will be like God, knowing good and evil." Gen 3:4-5 Man was lied to, just look around and you will find cemeteries and tombs of those who have passed away, regardless of their origin. They did

The Helper: The Holy Spirit. Omubezi: Mwoyo Mutukuzu

Die. This same enemy, Satan, spreads wrong teachings about the things of God, it is a liar and in it there is no truth, Jesus brought out that point very well when He was dealing with those religious leaders who were against people becoming "born again" as well as knowing who God was. "You are of your father the devil, and the desire of your father you want to do. He was a murderer from the beginning and does not stand in the truth, because there is no truth in him. When he speaks a lie, he speaks from his own resources, for he is a liar and the father of it." John 8:44

We really need the help of the Holy Spirit!

We need the help of the Holy Spirit in every area of our lives; we need the Spirit of Wisdom to guide us and that is the Third Person of the Godhead. The old lie from Hell that you can live on earth just depending on you and others is an accident going somewhere to happen; the teaching that you do not need the Baptism of the Holy Spirit with evidence of Speaking in Tongues is incorrect and self-centered: it is intended by the devil to render you powerless and directionless, so that you just stagger through life and get run over by demons, as well as taken advantage of, by Satan and forces of wickedness.

The Holy Spirit; the Third Person of the Godhead

You have to have power and wisdom; Jesus Christ's words must be heeded to. "But you shall receive power when the Holy Spirit has come upon you; and you shall be witnesses to Me in Jerusalem, and in all Judea and Samaria, and to the end of the earth." Acts 1:8

The purpose of this book is to point out to you the right way to proceed in divine help through the Helper, the Holy Spirit – The Spirit of Wisdom. With His help, one gets to know what has been freely given to you, "Now we have received not the spirit of the world, but the Spirit who is from God, that we might know the things that have been freely given to us by God." I Cor 2:12

The Word of God, in the Bible, is God's will for His people. All of us can know the truth, the Word of God carries the wisdom of God and from it we learn righteousness; it is the Third Person of the Godhead who helps us to receive God's word. He is the Spirit of Wisdom, He operated in the life of Jesus Christ himself, while He was here on earth. "The Spirit of the LORD shall rest upon Him, The Spirit of wisdom and understanding, the Spirit of counsel and might. The Spirit of knowledge and of the fear of the Lord." Is 11:2

The Helper: The Holy Spirit. Omubezi: Mwoyo Mutukuvu

A Spirit Filled Life

A spirit filled life, glorifies Jesus Christ, and is word of God centered, for the greatest desire of the Holy Spirit is to reveal Jesus Christ to the world. A life that is empowered by the Holy Spirit tends to like what Jesus Christ the Son of God likes; that none should perish but all come to the knowledge of God Almighty. Jesus said in the Gospel of John, Chapter Sixteen, verse Fourteen, "He will glorify Me, for He will take of what is Mine and declare it to you." John 16:14

The Spirit filled life embraces the Gifts of the Holy Spirit, it does not run away from them, for that life is full of compassion and a desire to do good works; that life desires more people to be healed and set free and knows that it is impossible to help without the help of the Holy Spirit. When we say, 'Spirit Filled' we imply a life that is willing to be led by the Spirit of God, someone who understands that without Jesus Christ they can do nothing, "I am the vine, you are the branches. He who abides in Me, and I in him, bears much fruit, for without me, you can do nothing. "John 15:5

The Holy Spirit; the Third Person of the Godhead

My Christian Journey to Where I Am Now, in light of this Subject

I found myself in a family of people who were of the Catholic Religion, my father was involved in the activities of that church, he was part of the choir in a Cathedral at Kitovu, Masaka, which was the seat of the Archdioceses in that area. This Diocese oversaw a number of parishes in that region of Uganda, Africa. His brother was the choir director at Butenda Catholic Parish in Masaka, Uganda. In fact, he composed a number of praise songs in the Catholic Church.

My grandfather, Leo Magala gave his sons very interesting names, to my father he gave Deogracious which means that God is gracious, to his brother he gave the name Deosidadit, which means, God is the Savior. He was a very religious man, as well as a great reader. He could memorize entire books, that were used for study, as well as worship in that denomination. Many times during various Catholic Church events, as well as family gatherings, he would be given a moment to recite word for word chapters of religious books, to astonishment of so many. He had an amazing memory.

The Helper: The Holy Spirit. Omubazi: Mwoyo Mutukuvu

God had given him an amazing gift, he could recite places in a book word to word, line to line, without looking at it. He could remember things in details with laser focused details, some thought he had a photographic mind. he could tell the progression of the Catholic Church popecy and that enabled me to understand better the historical aspects of the Catholic Church. He would tell those stories as if he lived among those people. He was also very good at telling the story of Jesus, and he was a very curious man. I was able to preach to him, Jesus Christ and I had him confess after me for the salvation of his soul. He was over 100 years old then, when I spoke to him. I had just returned from China, full of the Holy Spirit and ready to talk to anybody about the love of our Lord Jesus Christ, and thanks to God, I was able to talk to Grandpa, and he honored the message of Our Lord Jesus Christ, and received Him as his personal savior that day.

I found myself in that religion to begin with.

Like many people on earth, I took on what I found with my parents – that was the Catholic Religion. Growing up, I used to wear a rosary, that is a necklace

The Holy Spirit; the Third Person of the Godhead

with many beads on it with a cross attached to it. I was taught early in life that God is real and He is the one who created us. I was also told that God is the final judge of all the earth, also then in that religion they told us that there was Hell fire prepared for those who are not willing to obey the Ten Commandments, in fact, early in our growth, each one of us in that religion then, were taught the Ten Commandments, and we had to know them by heart, you had to be able to recite them, guess what? My Grandpa used to teach us the young ones, to recite the Ten Commandments.

Afraid of Hell Fire

I had been around fire, I noticed what it could do, plus cooking our food daily, I had also noticed as a child that fire could burn. I knew people who had fire burns, and what pain then, they had to go through, I had observed fire burning houses to the ground, as well as forests. So when I was told that there is fire in Hell, I purposed in my heart to never go to Hell, there were also some friends of mine who as well, were trying their best to avoid Hell fire!!! The only way how we knew how to do it them, was to try our best to be faithful to the religions we found ourselves in. A number of my

The Helper: The Holy Spirit. Omubezi: Mwoyo Mutukuvu

friends from different religious beliefs would disagree on a number of doctrinal issues, but most of them had this belief in common: 'that there is fire in Hell,' and no well-informed person would like to go there. I bet if any of them had an opportunity to know better, they would have reconsidered their stand, religiously.

I Become an Altar Boy

When the Catholic Cathedral near our primary school; that is St. Peter's Primary School, Nsambya, in the capital city of Uganda, Kampala, needed Altar boys to help serve in the church services, my name was suggested to the Priest, by our teacher. They told them that I and three other students were God lovers. I was about nine years of age at that time. My parents gave me a, go ahead on realizing that I was very willing to serve God, so they gave a big, 'Yes' to the church.

I Had a Dream About Hell

For some reason, one night when I went to sleep, I found myself looking over the horizon, and what I saw was a sea of fire, it was like liquid fire boiling over, up and down, and out there I could see forms of human

The Holy Spirit; the Third Person of the Godhead

beings chained and in agony, trying to get up, to free themselves from the Hell fires they were in. But those chains could not let them go. They were so many in number drowning in Hell fire; I woke up speechless and terrified. I was sweating all over and trembling. That dream came to me when I was about twelve years of age, what I saw never left my memory. To me, Hell was real, and I did not want to have anything to do with it. I have heard of people having visions of Jesus Christ coming and talking with them, especially, this has been going on in Arab nations, it also happens with people in other places. Other people have had different experiences, they have experienced visions of Heaven and had amazing Dreams, which have led them to seek God and in the process, they have found salvation. The Bible says in the Book of Joel, "And it shall come to pass afterward That I will pour out My Spirit on all flesh; Your sons and your daughters shall prophesy, Your old men shall dream dreams, Your young men shall see visions." Joel 2:28 Thank God for the Holy Spirit, He is really a present Help, even through dreams and visions. Maybe you are not yet born again, but you have been having experiences of God visions and you have been wondering why this is happening to you. I would like to let you know that God is trying to get your

The Helper: The Holy Spirit. Omubezi: Mwoyo Mutukuvu

attention, Christianity is a lifestyle, it is about relationship, the Kingdom of God is a family of those who have accepted Jesus Christ as their personal savior, it is not a religion. God reveals Himself to all of us in various ways, regardless of our religion, and the objective here is to draw us to His Word in the Holy Bible that points to the Savior Jesus Christ. In case you had some doubt about the extent of the love of God, I would like to inform you that God loves you so much that by His Holy Spirit, He can convict you about sin, and then point you to the right direction. That is also why this book has been written, under the leading of the Holy Spirit.

Serving in the Catholic Church as an Altar Boy

I would attend almost every Mass at St. Peter's Cathedral, Nsambya in Uganda, every day after school. I would be in the evening services, going before the priests, and helping them with the service. I would help with serving Holy Communion and many times there would be four of us serving at the altar. We rang the bells, held out the vulgate to the priests, as they read the scriptures, we did all that was requested of us. Your brother, Bishop Leonard Kayiwa, is shedding light on

The Holy Spirit; the Third Person of the Godhead

his Christian journey to help you understand that you can get a turn around by the help of the Holy Spirit from your deep religious practices. It does not matter how deep you are in there, but what matters is your willingness to be helped. I was so deep in religion that it had to take divine intervention for me to switch from religious rituals to relationship with God, and God did it for me. He can do it for you also.

You might be of the Jehovah Witness religion; Buddhism; Hinduism; Islam; Mormon; Atheism; the I Am Religion; of Sigh Religion, etc., the Lord God who pulled me out of the religious situation I was in is pulling you out of the clutches of that system right now, for God loves you, and wants the best for you. The only way is Jesus Christ. No one can come to God except through Him. "Jesus said to him, "I am the way, the truth, and the life. No one comes to the Father except through Me." John 14:6

In this book, about the Holy Spirit, the Third Person of the Godhead, we are not trying to criticize anyone in regard to their religion. Our task is to bring you in the right way, which is very well laid out in the Holy Scriptures – the Bible; that way is Jesus Christ.

The Helper: The Holy Spirit. Omubezi: Mwoyo Mutukuvu

In my religion then, they never instructed us to read Bibles

I never had a Holy Bible, we then were told by the priests in that religion that for us to be faithful to the church, we had to abide by the Catholic Doctrine; that it was not wise for us to read the Bible for ourselves or else we would be confused. We were told that it was the duty of the priest in that religion to interpret as well as read the Bible for us.

I had various other books for my different subjects at school, teachers had a copy and we students had copies of our own, even in all of the colleges that I attended, they all emphasized that we the students, we had to have the books that were part of the curriculum in any subject taught in order for us to make good grades. Our parents were required to buy text books that went along with the different subjects. What is amazing, when it came to the subject 'God' we were told by the priests that we did not need to have a Bible!!! Maybe it is worse than this in the religion where you are right now, the fact that even the word Bible is not mentioned in your gatherings. Well, it is time to move.

The Holy Spirit; the Third Person of the Godhead

I could see some other Christians of a different denomination carrying the Holy Bible, and I would wonder why it was so; I went and asked a Bishop in the Catholic Church I was attending, about that. He just looked at me and smiled, saying 'they do not trust their priests, that is why they carry that book with them when they go to church, so that they may compare what he says, to what is in the Bible.' He went further to tell me, 'that we in our denomination we are highly qualified in the things of God, we have P.H.D.'s from our seminaries and universities, we can be trusted. You do not need to read the Bible for yourselves.'

I Get My First Bible, Miraculously

I was a student at St. Henry's College, Kitovu, Masaka in the nation of Uganda, Africa, busy preparing to become an engineer. I had done a number of subjects at the Ordinary Level, whereby you spend four years learning. I took Mathematics, Chemistry, Biology, Technical Drawing, Agriculture, History, English, Geography, Physics, Religious Studies, French and Accounting. This level of learning would compare to part of the high school in the United States of America.

The Helper: The Holy Spirit Omubezi: Mwoyo Mutukuvu

We had text books for all of these subjects, I also did literature. I used to score very, very high by God's grace. I know that the Holy Spirit helped me. There was something unusual by me, that could enable me to do very well at school, even the teachers acknowledged that. Because one is not born again, it does not mean that they can't get help from God. There is so much evidence that God puts before a human being witnesses to help them turn to God, and the Holy Spirit is key in that. You would not know God without the Holy Spirit, the Third Person of the Godhead revealing Him to you. Even for you to have this book in your hand, it took God Himself.

I was still a student, full of curiosity, when I heard one of the wives of my uncle, who was Catholic narrate that there was a fellowship of tongue speaking, Holy Spirit filled believers, in a town within the City of Kampala called, Nnankulabya, in Uganda, Africa. She said, miracles, wonders and signs were happening among those people. When I heard that, I was still a teenager with great dreams and aspirations, and I was involved in so much learning, what she said caught my attention right away for the religion I was part of, there were no tangible miracles nor wonders and signs at all.

The Holy Spirit; the Third Person of the Godhead

You walk in those churches sick, you come out still sick; when someone walks in under demonic spells, they walk out still under the influence of witchcraft and sorcery. I never saw any priest calling out people during the Mass to pray for them for healing or deliverance. Many times one could not tell the difference between the Christians in those churches and the people of other religions, worse; the nonbelievers! They quarreled like people without hope, fought over everything. It was a time of political uncertainty, where many of these people were at one another's throat, cursing and getting drunk, intolerant, and very violent. It did not seem that there was any fundamental change in their lives, due to their religions. We all seemed like we needed to know God, a lot more.

I really wanted to know for myself, what was causing miracles and wonders to happen in those 'Born Again' believers' fellowship.

A Pastor Prays for Me and I Get My First Holy Bible

I went to the assembly of those Bible reading Christians, and as a young man, trained in examining specimen in the science laboratory at school, I watched and studied everything they said contrary to what I knew, I also tried to figure out what new religion was

-234-

The Helper: The Holy Spirit. Omubuzi: Mwoyo Mutukuvu

that. But what amazed me, everything they said, they referred to the book called, The Holy Bible. As a student I thought that these were very reasonable people and very fair minded, they were like the people of Berea in the book of Acts, "There the brethren immediately sent Paul and Silas away by night to Berea, when they arrived, they went into the synagogue of the Jews. These were more fair-minded than those in Thessalonica, in that they received the Word with all readiness and searched the scriptures daily to find out whether these things were so. Therefore, many of them believed, and also not a few of the Greeks, prominent women as well as men." Acts 17: 10-12

Miracles were happening in the Name of our Lord Jesus Christ; devils were leaving people's lives with a loud cry, it was very clear that there was supernatural power present in the service, something I could not refute.

The Preacher Prophecies to Me

Suddenly, the pastor pointed at me, I was way in the back of the room, with my body touching the back wall of the assembly hall. That man of God looked at me

The Holy Spirit; the Third Person of the Godhead

and said, God says: *'you shall be a minister of the Gospel of our Lord Jesus Christ, miracles, wonders and signs shall follow the Word that you preach and teach; many will be turned to the Love of God through the call on your life and you shall write a lot of inspiring Christian books for the Lord God, as well as build churches for Him, your Call will take you to nations.'*

When I heard all of that, I immediately responded to him and said, 'I am a Catholic.' He looked at me and smiled, saying, 'Do you have a Holy Bible?' I said no, we Catholics do not read Bibles, the Priest reads them for us. He said, today before you reach your home, you shall miraculously receive a Holy Bible; somebody will give you one and come with it to our next meeting, I will pray for you that you pass your national exams that are coming up.

Interesting enough, I was given a Bible by a man who never knew anything about what had transpired that day, it happened on my way as I was about to reach my place of residence. I loved that Bible, I called it 'a miracle Bible.' I started reading it and would place it under my pillow when I went to sleep. Well, I went

The Helper: The Holy Spirit. Omubezi: Mwoyo Mutukuzu

back to the Believer's Assembly with my miracle Bible and gave my testimony of how I received it. They praised the Lord and the Pastor and the whole congregation prayed for me, concerning the coming exams. I passed my exams, took on a combination called PCM; that is Physics, Mathematics, and Chemistry, with the intention of becoming an engineer. I was to be in that class for two years, it is referred to as the Advanced Level in Uganda, Africa, that is what you must do prior to entering a university, and that was at St. Henry's College, Kitovu.

Though I had seen all those miracles, I did not yet give my life to Jesus Christ as my Lord and Savior!! I was still holding onto my religion! It was as if I was caught up in a tug of war about what I was going to totally surrender to; either to the Catholic Religion or to the Person of Jesus Christ.

The Holy Spirit Helps Me to Become a 'Born Again' Christian

I never preach a Gospel of Condemnation, I'd rather be in line with the Holy Scriptures and operate in the

The Holy Spirit; the Third Person of the Godhead

ministerial of righteousness. My experience enabled me to know that religion is not just an institution, but it is something which the enemy can use to blind you to the person of our Savior Jesus Christ. When you are in it, you seem to be as if you are yoked to something, like something is holding on to you, it takes the Holy Spirit to convict you out of it. No wonder Jesus Christ, Our Lord and Savior said, "And when He has come, He will convict the world of sin, and of righteousness, and of judgment. "of sin because they do not believe in Me," John 16:8-9

I had been told that I was okay with my religion, I did not need to become 'born again'; a number of people of the Catholic Religion, who were my acquaintances then, explained to me with threats; that if I leave their denomination, they would disown me, and I will be doomed. But I had a witness inside me from God that I was going in the right direction, that religion alone could not fill the void in my heart, I needed Jesus Christ to be in the center of my life; the Holy Spirit was helping me.

I receive Jesus Christ as my Lord and Savior at Makerere University in Lumumba Hall, Uganda, Africa

The Helper: The Holy Spirit. Omubezi: Mwoyo Mutukuvu

I joined Makerere University for further studies, during very turbulent times, war was going on in the country of Uganda, one group was in the bush fighting, trying to remove those who were then in power. It was tough, and gun fights were everywhere, there was much uncertainty then among the people; Uganda needed a miracle from God. These levels of instability had affected a number of students, some never did very well with their exams due to too much anxiety and family deaths. Gun fire engulfed the nation; others had been displaced from their homes and had lost some of their dear relatives to war. I knew students who used to score very high in college, but because of infights in the government, many of them could not perform at their best in school. The truth is, all of us were affected negatively. We all needed a true savior!

I happened to visit my fellow students at the university residince in a different hall. My residence was Mitchell Hall, they were staying in Lumumba Hall, the moment I stepped in their room, one of them who knew me from our previous college, said this, 'Leonard is a very religious person, he loves God, but he needs to become 'Born Again'; I know he would do wonders if

The Holy Spirit; the Third Person of the Godhead

he was born again.' That caught my attention right away, for up to that time, I had never confessed Jesus Christ as my Lord and Savior as it should be done according to Romans Chapter Ten, Verse Nine. "that if you confess with your mouth the Lord Jesus and believe in your heart that God has raised Him from the dead, you will be saved. For with the heart one believes unto righteousness, and with the mouth confession is made unto salvation." Rom 10:9-10

Implication of the Word Confession

The word confession, in the religion that I was in then, mostly meant to say the things you have done wrong to the priest in the confession chamber at church. It was never looked at as a way to receive a new life in Christ, any time that word was used, it was about confessing sins.

Well, I asked my fellow students what I needed to do to become a born again Christian. They gladly showed me that scripture in the book of Romans. We all knelt down and I repeated after them the words they said for me to invite Jesus Christ into my life, as my Lord and Savior; that day, I got on the right path in my life, left that religion alone, and became a strong follower of our resurrected Lord and Savior Jesus Christ.

The Helper: The Holy Spirit. Omubezi: Mwoyo Mutukuvu

I am a believer, not a doubter; I am a 'Born Again' Christian, and part of the world wide Body of disciples of our Lord Jesus Christ. We are on the way to Heaven, not Hell. I don't like Hell, I want to spend my eternity with God, so should you.

I further went ahead and received the Baptism of the Holy Spirit, with evidence of speaking in tongues. I have ministered to people from all kinds of religious backgrounds and I have done it with compassion, considering where God brought me from; for many are where they are in their brief system because of what was handed to them by their immediate relatives in their early upbringing. People do need help, we all need help to know the truth and that is the purpose and role of this book. We need to know the Holy Spirit, the Third Person of the Godhead.

There is more in God, only let God reveal to you more through His word. Many of those I have seen who have taken the right road in Christ, were deep in religions that taught a form of godliness, but denied the power of God. Religions talking about God's power while you see none of it in their midst, religions talking about the gifts of the Holy Spirit while at the same time, reject them, those groups that say, with God all things

The Holy Spirit; the Third Person of the Godhead

are possible, but turn around and say that God cannot have a son, and there are some others which say, it is alright to become Born Again, but you do not need the Holy Spirit, neither the Baptism of the Holy Spirit with evidence of speaking in tongues. "Having a form of godliness but denying its power. And from such people turn away!" 2 Tim 3:5 Please turn to God Almighty and love God's people, and embrace God's Son, Jesus Christ; let the Holy Spirit guide you and lead you, for you are a Child of God. "For as many as are led by the Spirit of God, these are the sons of God." Rom 8:14

Once I became born again, the Holy Spirit led me to join churches where the Word of God was preached and taught under the anointing. I started early after conversion, to go after the Word of God. He guided me to places where the Saints loved worshiping God in the Spirit and the Truth. "God is Spirit and those who worship Him, must worship in spirit and truth." John 4:24 I became a student of the Bible, took time to read spiritual books written by anointed authors; those who are God sent, with a word of life from the Spirit of God

The Helper: The Holy Spirit. Omubezi: Mwoyo Mutukuvu

Godly, anointed men and women to teach others as well as present the Word of God to the hurting world with grace and compassion.

Beloved: The Holy Spirit; the third person of the Godhead; The Helper

The Comforter

The Spirit of Truth

The Spirit of Wisdom

The Spirit of the Fear of the Lord

The Spirit of Understanding

The Spirit of Counsel

The Teacher

Spirit of God

Spirit of Christ

God

Jehovah-Shammah

The Lord is

Present

Please be a partner to this ministry by sowing your seed in this good ground, that we may get this message to as many as possible.

Honor the Lord with your possessions and with the first fruits of all your increase; so your barns will be filled with plenty, and your vats will overflow with new wine.   Proverbs 3:9-10

**Many have done that and God
Has healed them miraculously**

Leonard Kayiwa Ministries

P.O. Box 1898

Bolingbrook, Illinois 60440

(224)440-6992

kayiwaministries@yahoo.com

Follow us on Face Book:

Bishop Leonard Kayiwa

Other books written by the author:

1. Ministering to God, Key to a Prosperous Life/Church filled with God's Power, Miracles, Wonders and Signs

2. Receive Your Healing in the Name of Jesus Christ of Nazareth

3. You Can Prosper in God

4. What Happens when we Pray and Believe God

5. The Most Powerful People on Earth Revealed

www.ministeringtogod.com

THE ISAIAH 58 BLESSING:

You can also receive a copy of this book for a donation of $30.00 or more in support of the drive to help orphans.

Bishop Leonard MP Kayiwa founded a 501©3 tax exempt church organization for helping orphans in different countries in Africa.

This organization is registered in the U.S.A. and in Africa. It is called:

AFRICAN CHILDREN BENEVOLENCE FOUNDATION INTERNATIONAL, INC.

We shall send you a tax-deductible receipt for your gift towards helping God's children – the orphans.

We will also send you a copy of this beautiful book.

Make your check payable to:

A.C.B.F.I., Inc. or African Children Benevolence Foundation International, Inc.

P.O. Box 1898, Bolingbrook, IL 60440

www.acbfii.org; www.ministeringtogod.com

acbfii@yahoo.com   God bless you!!!

"In the beginning God created the heavens and the earth. The earth was without form, and void; and darkness was on the face of the deep. And the Spirit of God was hovering over the face of the waters. Then God said, "Let there be light"; and there was light." Gen 1:1-3

"For this is good and acceptable in the sight of God our Savior, who desires all men to be saved and to come to the knowledge of the truth. For there is one God and one Mediator between God and men, the Man Christ Jesus, who gave Himself a ransom for all, to be testified in due time," I Timothy 2:3-6

"But what does it say? "The word is near you, in your mouth and in your heart (that is, the word of faith which we preach): that if you confess with your mouth the Lord Jesus and believe in your heart that God has raised Him from the dead, you will be saved. For with the heart one believes unto righteousness, and with the mouth confession is made unto salvation. For the Scripture says, "Whoever believes on Him will not be put to shame." Romans 10:8-11

Quotations in the English Language

"But as many as received Him, to them He gave the right to become children of God, to those who believe in His name: who were born, not of blood, nor of the will of the flesh, nor of the will of man, but of God." John 1:12-13

Jesus answered and said to him, "most assuredly, I say to you, unless one is born again, he cannot see the kingdom of God. " John 3:3

"Ekyo kye kirungi, ekikkirizibwa mu maaso g"Omulokozi waffe Katonda, 4 ayagala abantu bonna okulokoka, era okutuuka mu kutegeerera ddala amazima. 5 Kubanga waliwo Katonda omu, era omutabaganya wa Katonda n"abantu omu, omuntu Kristo Yesu, 6 eyeewaayo abe omutango olwa bonna; okutegeeza kulibaawo mu ntuuko zaakwo:" 1Timoseewo 2:3-6

This is Luganda language (Uganda) Africa

"Naye bwogera butya? Nti, Ekigambo kiri kumpi naawe, mu kamwa ko, ne mu mutima gwo: kye kigambo eky'okukkiriza kye tubuulira: 9 kubanga bw'oyatula Yesu nga ye Mukama n'akamwa ko, n'okkiriza mu mutima gwo nti Katonda yamuzuukiza mu bafu, olirokoka: 10 kubanga omuntu akkiriza na mutima okuweebwa obutuukirivu, era ayatula na kamwa okulokoka." Abaruumi 10:8-10

"Naye bonna abaamusembeza yabawa obuyinza okufuuka abaana ba Katonda, be bakkiriza erinnya lye" Yokkaana 1:12

Write your testimony here, how you became 'Born Again'

3 Hili ni zuri, nalo lakubalika mbele za Mungu Mwokozi wetu;

4 ambaye hutaka watu wote waokolewe, na kupata kujua yaliyo kweli.

5 Kwa sababu Mungu ni mmoja, na mpatanishi kati ya Mungu na wanadamu ni mmoja, Mwanadamu Kristo Yesu;

6 ambaye alijitoa mwenyewe kuwa ukombozi kwa ajili ya wote, utakaoshuhudiwa kwa majira yake. 1 Timotheo Mlango 2:3-6

Swahili Language, Africa

8 Lakini yanenaje? Lile neno li karibu nawe, katika kinywa chako, na katika moyo wako; yaani, ni lile neno la imani tulihubirilo.
9 Kwa sababu, ukimkiri Yesu kwa kinywa chako ya kuwa ni Bwana, na kuamini moyoni mwako ya kuwa Mungu alimfufua katika wafu, utaokoka.
10 Kwa maana kwa moyo mtu huamini hata kupata haki, na kwa kinywa hukiri hata kupata wokovu. Warumi Mlango 10: 8-10

12 Bali wote waliompokea aliwapa uwezo wa kufanyika watoto wa Mungu, ndio wale waliaminio jina lake; Yohana Mlango 1: 12

Make sure

You receive

The Baptism

Of the Holy Spirit

With evidence

Of

Speaking

In Tongues

"However, when He, the Spirit of truth, has come, He will guide

John 16:13

3   这是好的，在神我们救主面前可蒙悦纳。

4   他愿意万人得救，明白真道。

5 因为只有一位神，在神和人中间，只有一位中保，乃是降世为人的基督耶稣。

6 他舍自己作万人的赎价。到了时候，这事必证明出来。   提

摩太前书 2 章 3-6

8 他到底怎么说呢？他说，这道离你不远，正在你口里，在你心里。就是我们所传信主的道。

9   你若口里认耶稣为主，心里信神叫他从死里复活，就必得救。

10 因为人心里相信，就可以称义。口里承认，就可以得救。 罗

马书 10 章 8-10

12 凡接待他的，就是信他名的人，他就赐他们权柄，作神的儿女。 約

翰福音 1 章 12

Chinese Language

Following, is The Lord's Prayer in 12 languages

of

the world.

14 For as many as are led by the Spirit of God, these are sons of God.

15 For you did not receive the spirit of bondage again to fear, but you received the Spirit of adoption by whom we cry out, "Abba, Father."

16 The Spirit Himself bears witness with our spirit that we are children of God,

17 and if children, then heirs--heirs of God and joint heirs with Christ, if indeed we suffer with Him, that we may also be glorified together.

18 For I consider that the sufferings of this present time are not worthy to be compared with the glory which shall be revealed in us.

19 *For the earnest expectation of the creation eagerly waits for the revealing of the sons of God.*

20 For the creation was subjected to futility, not willingly, but because of Him who subjected it in hope;

The Lord's Prayer in English

[8] "Therefore do not be like them. For your Father knows the things you have need of before you ask Him. [9] In this manner, therefore, pray:
Our Father in heaven,
Hallowed be Your name.
[10] Your kingdom come.
Your will be done
On earth as it is in heaven.
[11] Give us this day our daily bread.
[12] And forgive us our debts,
As we forgive our debtors.
[13] And do not lead us into temptation,
But deliver us from the evil one.
For Yours is the kingdom and the power and the glory forever. Amen.[b]

[14] "For if you forgive men their trespasses, your heavenly Father will also forgive you. [15] But if you do not forgive men their trespasses, neither will your Father forgive your trespasses. Matt 6:8-15

THE LORD'S PRAYER IN CHINESE

8 **不可像他**们那样，因为在你们祷告以前，你们的父已经知道你们的需要了。

9 **"你们应当这样祷告，**

" '**我们天上的父，**

愿人们都尊崇你的圣名，

10 **愿你的国度降**临，

愿你的旨意在地上成就，就像在天上成就一样。

11 **求你今天**赐给我们日用的饮食。

12 **饶恕我们的罪，**

就像我们饶恕了得罪我们的人。

13 **不要**让我们遇见诱惑，

救我们脱离那恶者。

因为国度、权柄、荣耀都是你的，直到永远。阿们！'

14 **"如果你**们饶恕别人的过犯，你们的天父也必饶恕你们的过犯。 15 **如果你**们不饶恕别人的过犯，你们的天父也不会饶恕你们的过犯。

THE LORD'S PRAYER IN SWAHILI

[8] Msiwe kama wao, kwa sababu Baba yenu anajua mahitaji yenu hata kabla hamjaomba." [9] Basi msalipo ombeni hivi: 'Baba yetu uliye mbinguni jina lako litukuzwe.[10] Ufalme wako uje, mapenzi yako yafanyike hapa duniani kama huko mbinguni. [11] Utupatie leo riziki yetu ya kila siku. [12] Na utusamehe makosa yetu kama sisi tulivyokwisha kuwa samehe waliotukosea. [13] Na usitutie majaribuni, bali utuokoe kutokana na yule mwovu,' [Kwa kuwa Ufalme na nguvu na utukufu ni vyako milele. Amina.] [14] Kama mkiwasamehe watu makosa yao, Baba yenu wa mbinguni atawasamehe na ninyi; [15] lakini msipowasamehe watu makosa yao, Baba yenu hatawasamehe makosa yenu.

THE LORD'S PRAYER IN RUSSIAN

⁸ Не уподобляйтесь им, потому что Отец ваш знает, в чём вы нуждаетесь, прежде чем вы попросили его об этом. ⁹ А потому молитесь вот как:

„Отец наш Небесный,
    да будет свято имя Твоё.
¹⁰ Да наступит Царство Твоё.
    Пусть исполнится воля Твоя на земле,
    как и на Небе.
¹¹ Пошли нам хлеб насущный на каждый день
¹² и прости нам грехи наши,
    как мы простили тех, кто причинил нам зло.
¹³ Не подвергай нас искушению,
    но избавь нас от лукавого"
[Так как Тебе принадлежат и Царство,
    и сила, и Слава вовеки. Аминь.] [a

¹⁴ Потому что если вы простите людей за их грехи, то и Отец ваш Небесный тоже простит вам. ¹⁵ Если же вы не простите тех, кто причинил вам зло, то и Отец ваш не простит ваши грехи».

⁸ 너희는 그들을 본받지 말아라. 너희 아버지께서는 너희가 구하기 전에 너희에게 필요한 것이 무엇인지 다 알고 계신다.

⁹ 그러므로 너희는 이렇게 기도하여라. '하늘에 계신 우리 아버지, 아버지의 이름이 거룩히 여김을 받게 하시고

¹⁰ 아버지의 나라가 속히 오게 하소서. 아버지의 뜻이 하늘에서 이루어진 것같이 땅에서도 이루어지게 하소서.

¹¹ 우리에게 날마다 필요한 양식을 주시고

¹² 우리가 우리에게 죄 지은 사람들을 용서해 준 것처럼 우리 [a]죄를 용서해 주소서.

¹³ 우리가 시험에 들지 않게 하시고 우리를 [b]악에서 구해 주소서. [c](나라와 권세와 영광이 영원토록 아버지의 것입니다. 아멘.)'

¹⁴ "너희가 다른 사람의 죄를 용서하면 하늘에 계신 너희 아버지께서도 너희를 용서하실 것이다.

¹⁵ 그러나 너희가 다른 사람의 죄를 용서하지 않으면 너희 아버지께서도 너희 죄를 용서하지 않으실 것이다

THE LORD'S PRAYER IN KOREAN

THE LORD'S PRAYER IN ARABIC

أَباكُمْ لِأَنَّ ،مِثلَهُمْ تَكُونُوا لا لِذَلِكَ 8. كَلامِهِمْ كَثْرَةِ
تَطلُبُوهُ أَنْ قَبلَ حَتَّى إِلَيهِ تَحتاجُونَ ما يَعرِفُ
:يَلِي كَما صَلُّوا لِذَلِكَ 9. مِنهُ

،السَّماءِ فِي الَّذِي أبانا〉
،اسْمُكَ لِيَتَقَدَّس
،مَلَكُوتُكَ لِيَأتِ 10
،مَشِيئَتُكَ فَتَكُونَ
.السَّماءِ فِي هِيَ كَما الأرْضِ عَلَى هُنا
،يَومِنا كَفافَ خُبزَنا اليَومَ أعطِنا 11
،خَطايانا لَنا وَاغفِرْ 12
.إلَينا يُسِيئُونَ لِلَّذِينَ أيضاً نَحنُ غَفَرْنا كَما
،تَجرُبَةٍ فِي تُدْخِلنا وَلا 13
[a] .الشِّرِّيرِ مِنَ أنقِذْنا بَلْ
،وَالمَجدَ وَالقُدرَةَ المُلْكَ لَكَ لِأَنَّ
〈آمين .الآبدِينَ أبَدِ إلَى

تَغفِرُوا لَمْ إنْ لَكِنْ 15. أيضاً السَّماوِيُّ أبوكُمْ لَكُمْ يَغفِرْ ،زَلّاتِهِمْ لِلنّاسِ غَفَرْتُمْ إنْ لِأَنَّكُمْ 14
.زَلّاتِكُمْ أبوكُمْ لَكُمْ يَغفِرَ فَلَنْ ،زَلّاتِهِمْ لِلآخَرِينَ

8 No sean como ellos, porque su Padre ya sabe lo que ustedes necesitan, antes que se lo pidan. **9** Ustedes deben orar así:

»"Padre nuestro que estás en el cielo, santificado sea tu nombre.
10 Venga tu reino.
Hágase tu voluntad en la tierra, así como se hace en el cielo.
11 Danos hoy el pan que necesitamos.
12 Perdónanos el mal que hemos hecho,
así como nosotros hemos perdonado a los que nos han hecho mal.
13 No nos expongas a la tentación, sino líbranos del maligno."

14 »Porque si ustedes perdonan a otros el mal que les han hecho, su Padre que está en el cielo los perdonará también a ustedes; **15** pero si no perdonan a otros, tampoco su Padre les perdonará a ustedes sus pecados.

⁸ Ne les imitez pas, car votre Père sait ce qu'il vous faut, avant que vous le lui demandiez.

(Lc 11.2-4) THE LORD'S PRAYER IN

⁹ Priez donc ainsi: FRENCH
Notre Père,
qui es aux cieux,
que ton nom soit sanctifié[a],
¹⁰ que ton règne vienne,
que ta volonté soit faite,
sur la terre comme au ciel.
¹¹ Donne-nous aujourd'hui
le pain dont nous avons besoin[b],
¹² pardonne-nous nos torts envers toi
comme nous aussi, nous pardonnons
les torts des autres envers nous[c].
¹³ Ne nous expose pas à la tentation[d],
et surtout, délivre-nous du diable[e].
[Car à toi appartiennent
le règne et la puissance
et la gloire à jamais[f].]

¹⁴ En effet, si vous pardonnez aux autres leurs fautes, votre Père céleste vous pardonnera aussi. ¹⁵ Mais si vous ne pardonnez pas aux autres, votre Père ne vous pardonnera pas non plus vos fautes.

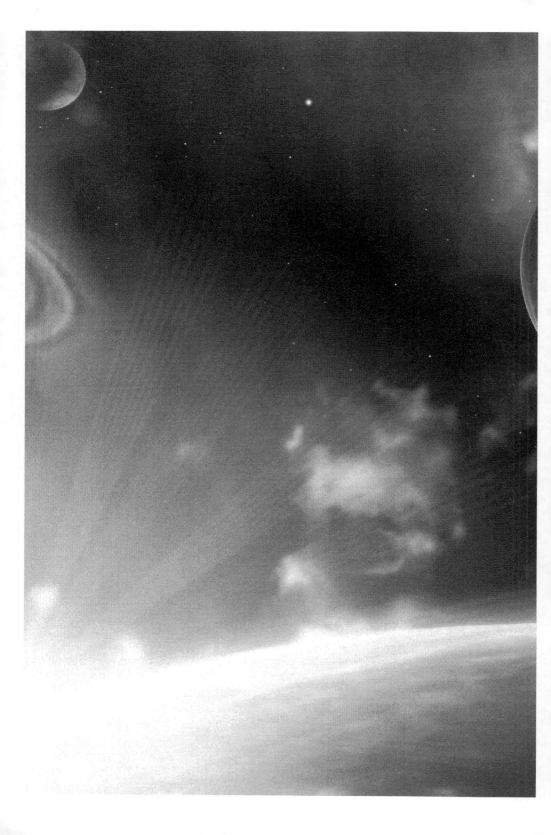

⁸ Sidaa darteed ha ahaanina sidooda oo kale, waayo, Aabbihiin waa og yahay waxaad u baahan tihiin intaanad weyddiin. **THE LORD'S**

Tukashaduu Ciise Xertiisii Baray

⁹ Haddaba sidatan u tukada, Aabbahayaga jannada ku jirow, magacaagu quduus ha ahaado. ¹⁰ Boqortooyadaadu ha timaado, doonistaada dhulka ha lagu yeelo sida jannada loogu yeelo. ¹¹ Kibis maalin nagu filan, maanta na sii. ¹² Oo naga cafi qaamahayaga sidaannu u cafinnay kuwa noo qaamaysan. ¹³ Oo jirrabaadda ha noo kaxayn, laakiin sharka naga du. Waayo, boqortooyada iyo xoogga iyo ammaanta adigaa leh weligaa. Aamiin. **PRAYER IN SOMALI**

¹⁴ Waayo, haddaad dadka u cafidaan xumaantooda, Aabbihiinna jannada ku jira ayaa idin cafiyi doona. ¹⁵ Laakiin haddaanad dadka cafiyin, Aabbihiinnu xumaantiinna idiin cafiyi maayo.

THE LORD'S PRAYER IN LUGANDA

8 Kale, temufaanana nga bo: kubanga Kitammwe amanyi bye mwetaaga nga temunnaba kumusaba.

9 Kale, musabenga bwe muti, nti, Kitaffe a1i ggulu, Erinnya lyo litukuzibwe.

10 Obwakabaka bwo bujje. By'oyagala bikolebwe mu nsi, nga bwe bikolebwa mu ggulu.

11 Otuwe leero emmere yaffe eya leero.

12 Otusonyiwe amabanja gaffe, nga naffe bwe tusonyiye abatwewolako.

13 Totutwala mu kukemebwa, naye otulokole eri omubi. Kubanga obwakabaka, n'obuyinza, n'ekitiibwa, bibyo, emirembe n'emirembe, Amiina.

14 Kubanga bwe munaasonyiwanga abantu ebyonoono byabwe, Kitammwe ali mu ggulu anaabasonyiwanga nammwe.

15 Naye bwe mutaasonyiwenga bantu ebyonoono byabwe, ne Kitammwe taasonyiwenga byonoono byammwe.

THE LORD'S PRAYER IN YORUBA

Baba wa ti mbẹ li ọrun

Ki a bọwọ fun orukọ rẹ

Ki Ijọba rẹ de

Ifẹ tire ni ki a ṣe

Bi ti orun, beni li aiye

Fun wa li onje Ojo wa loni

Dari gbese wa ji wa

Bi awa ti ndariji awon onigbese wa

Ma si fa wa sinu idewo

Sugbon gba wa lowo bilisi

Nitori ijo ba ni tire

Ati agbara, Ati ogo

OUR LORD'S PRAYER (IGBO)

West Africa

Nna anyi bi n'igwe
ka aha gi di nso
ka Ala eze gi bia
ka anyi mee ihe i nacho
dika esi ème Ya n'igwe
nye anyi Taa
nke Ga ezuru anyi ubochi taa
gbaghara anyi njor anyi niile
etu anyi si gbaghara ndi meghere anyi
e dubele anyi n'Ime onwunwa
gbaputa anyi n'Aka ajor ihe
n'ihi n'Ala eze bu nke gi
na ike na otuto Mgbe niile oge niile
Amen

WRITE HERE THE LORD'S
PRAYER
IN YOUR LANGUAGE

The Word 'The Holy Spirit' in various languages

I神圣的灵魂 in Chinese

An Spiorad Naomh in Scottish Gaelic

Der Heilige Geist in German

الروح القدس

In Arabic

An Spiorad Naomh in Irish

רוח הקודש

In Hebrew

Το Άγιο Πνεύμα in Greek

聖霊 in Japanese

RCвятой Дух in Russian

SwahRoho Mtakatifu in Swahili

PDuch Święty in Polish

Den heliga anden in Swedish

Yemi Mimo in Yoruba

Святий Дух in Ukrainian

روح مقدس

in Persian

Ruuxa Quduuska ah in Somali

El espíritu santo in Spanish

Helligånden in Danish

FLe Saint-Esprit in French

Ruhu Mai Tsarki in Hausa

Zumoya oNgcwele in Zuru

Omwoyo Omutukuvu in Luganda

Kutsal Ruh in Turkish

Sentespri a in Haiten Creole

神聖的靈魂 in Traditional Chines

The Phrase "The 'born again' Christians"
in various language:-
ABALOKOLE in Luganda

ki fèt ankò kretyen yo in Haitian

tekrar doğdu christians in Turkish

waliozaliwa tena wa Kikristo in
Swahili

i cristiani di nuovo rinati in Italian

重生的基督徒 in Chinese

ولدوا مسيحيين

In Arabic

los cristianos nacidos de nuevo in
Spanish

les chrétiens nés de nouveau   in
French

рожденные свыше христиане   in
Russian

os cristãos nascidos de novo   in
Portuguese

נולד שוב נוצרים

in Hebrew

die wiedergeborenen Christen in
German

ndị a mụrụ ọzọ ndị Kraịst in   Igbo

de født igjen kristne in Norwegian

οι αναγεννημένοι χριστιανοί in
Greek

abazalwa kabusha abangamaKristu
in Zulu

de födda igen kristna   in Swedish

na Crìosdaidhean a rugadh a-rithist
in Scottish Gaelic

Become a Partner

Beloved, this ministry of the Written Word by our brother in Christ, requires your participation monetary wise.

This book was made possible through the giving and support of people like you, who desire the best for the people.

Their generosity has made this magnificent work available to the world.

Will you please, start giving to this ministry, please send a gift of support to enable this book and others to go to God lovers.

You may send your seed or monetary gift to:

Bishop Leonard KAYIWA

P.O. Box 1898

Bolingbrook, Illinois 60440

U.S.A.

You can also sow through the secure web site:

www.ministeringtogod.com

www.prayandbelieveGod.org

Bishop's email is:

kayiwaministries@yahoo.com

His wife, Pastor Gail Kayiwa's email

Is: mrsrev3@gmail.com

God will cause money to multiply back to you when you support this ministry

Normally we tell people to sow a seed of at least $30 in order to get a copy of this book.

We then ship the book to that person immediately.

People have been so gracious towards this mission that they have sown far beyond $30, which has made the shipping of our books easier.

We love you all. You may contact us for prayer. Our phone number is: 224-440-6992